REPORT WRITING
FOR
INCREASED CONVICTIONS

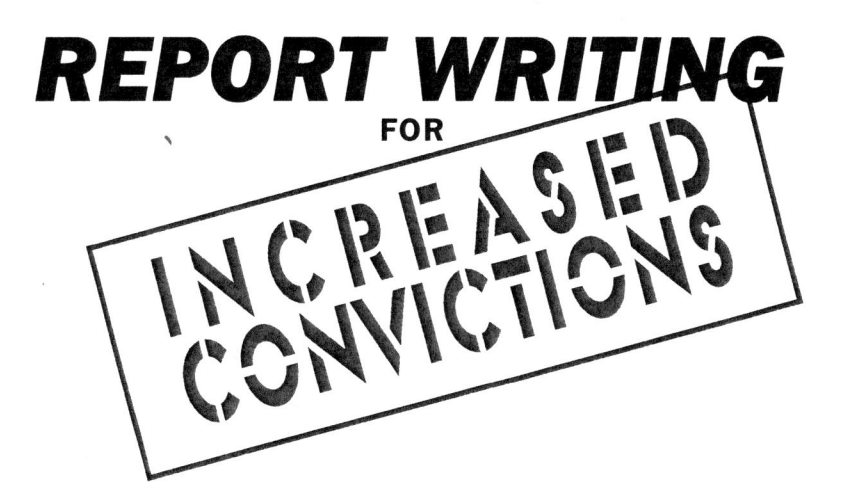

Produced by the
Law Enforcement Resource Center
in cooperation with:

Dean Berry Associates Inc.
Stan and Dean Berry

Hennepin County Attorney's Office, State of Minnesota
Fred Karasov, Assistant Hennepin County Attorney

Minnesota Program Development Inc.
Mary Asmus
Ellen Pence, Ph.D.
Michael Paymar

RoughEdge Consultants
Wesley Harris

© (2002/2017). Rev. ed. Law Enforcement Resource Center.

1515 Nicollet Avenue, Minneapolis, Minnesota 55403
Phone: 1-800-279-8284 ▶ **Fax:** (612) 872-0635 ▶ **E-mail:** info@lerc.com ▶ **Web:** www.lerc.com

LERC *Report Writing*

Many of the examples in this training have been taken from actual police reports. The names of all officers and suspects, places, and dates have been changed.

No portion of the information in this manual or website may be produced by any means, electronic or mechanical, including photography, recordings, or any information storage and retrieval now known or to be invented, without permission in written form from the Law Enforcement Resource Center.

© 2002 - 2017 Rev. ed. **Law Enforcement Resource Center**

Contents

Getting Started 1

Overview 3

"The Call" 5

Everyday Language 11

Writing Tips 25

Organization 37

Facts & Details 49

Legal Requirements 71

Writing the DUI/DWI Report 85

Writing the Domestic Violence Report 105

Answers to Exercises 122

Extras 130

Notes:

Getting Started

Report Writing is a hybrid online learning course. Part of your coursework will take place on the website: you will watch crime scene scenarios, complete interactive exercises and quizzes, and take a final exam. The other part of your coursework will be done in your workbook: you will write reports and correct and revise them as you go through the training. Follow these steps to get started:

1 *Connect to the internet.*

1. Go to **LERC.com**.
2. Select ONLINE CLASSES and click on "Login" for Report Writing for Increased Convictions.

The responsive design of the online course is "mobile friendly."

2 *Enter your e-mail and password to begin training.*
(Your password/code is on the inside cover of your workbook.)

If you have a question or need help getting started, call 1-800-279-8284 or e-mail info@lerc.com.
Hours are M-F 8:30 a.m. – 4:30 p.m. CST

LERC Report Writing

Getting Started

Before you start online training, make sure you:
- Have enough time to complete the chapter you have started. (Approximate times are posted at the beginning of each section.)
- Understand that it is to your advantage to complete all the exercises.
- Understand that you must complete the short quiz at the end of each online chapter to get credit for completing that chapter.

About the Workbook
The workbook parallels the online training. There is somewhat more information in the book than in the online version, and there is some variation in the exercises. You will use the workbook to take notes on the video scenarios, and to write and revise your reports. There is also a section of "EXTRAS" (page 130) that does not appear online. It contains sample reports and word guides for your reference.

At times during the online training you will be asked to refer back to the workbook. **It is in your best interest to read the workbook completely** and to complete all exercises, as all information is fair game for the post-test.

Keeping Track of Your Online Progress
Once you have completed a chapter and its quiz, the program automatically records your progress on the home page with a check mark, and prompts you to the next chapter. **You must complete the entire chapter to get credit for it. If you stop in the middle of a chapter, your progress will be saved.**

☑ Start
☑ Everyday Language
☑ Writing Tips
☑ Organization
☑ Facts & Details
☑ Legal Requirements
☑ DUI/DWI Report
☑ Domestic Violence
☑ Post-test

You must have all the chapters check-marked on the home page in order to take the post-test.

Don't worry about completing all the chapters in one sitting. After you leave a session, your results are automatically saved. When you log on again you'll see that the chapters you have completed remain checked.

(You can revisit any finished chapter for review before you take the post-test. This will not cause them to revert to an "unchecked" state.)

The Post-Test
To pass this course, you must score **100%** on the post-test. The post-test is a set of relevant questions randomly selected from a bank of test items. If you miss a question, you will be required to repeat the chapter it came from and retake the post-test. (The chapter or chapters you missed questions in will become unchecked again.)

Overview

COURSE OBJECTIVES

- Write reports that are more precise and more effective.
- Include more facts and meet legal requirements.
- Write a DUI/DWI report and examine a domestic violence report.

*A police report is a written record of facts that identifies the **who**, **what**, **where**, **when**, **how**, and **why** (if possible) of a given incident.*

Write reports that are more precise and more effective.
Why are you taking this course? You're probably great in the field, but writing reports is a big irritation. After all, you didn't go into law enforcement to become a writer. You're a person of action. You know how to do your job in a precise, organized, and legal way, but when you put it down on paper it becomes a mess.

You may have had perfectly good cases thrown out, not because the arrest was bad, but because your report let you down. You may even know some very good officers who have lost their jobs because of poor writing skills. Or, you may just think of report writing on a par with the average root canal.

We understand your frustration. Many people do not particularly enjoy words and writing. That's okay! This course is meant to take the pain out of the writing process. Your reports will be more precise, easier to read, easier to write, and more effective in gaining convictions.

Chapter 1 will help you write simple, concise sentences. You'll throw out the gobbledygook, and get rid of vague and confusing terms (like *gobbledygook*).

Chapter 2 will give you some writing tips to improve your grammar.

Chapter 3 will teach you how to organize your report.

Course Objectives

Include more facts and meet legal requirements.
A report which sticks to the facts and meets legal requirements helps prosecutors charge more cases, negotiate for better pleas, and ultimately **get more convictions**. And increasing convictions is the main goal of this course.

Chapter 4 will help you refine how you put facts in your report. You'll learn how to use specific language, how to separate facts from opinions, how and when to use direct quotes, and why it is so important not to jump to conclusions.

Chapter 5 will show you how to write a report so binding that defense attorneys will run from the room screaming, "We don't have a chance!" You'll learn how to write reports which will put more bad boys in jail. You'll look at legal definitions of crimes, understand the sequence of an arrest, and use a "legal checklist" when writing your reports.

Write a DUI/DWI report and examine a domestic violence report.
Chapter 6 will deal with the DUI/DWI report. You'll learn how to establish a legal basis for your actions, what the elements of a DUI/DWI arrest are, and what the format of a DUI/DWI report is. You'll watch a DUI/DWI stop and write a report. The skills you learn here will help get drunk drivers off the road.

Chapter 7 will deal with the always difficult domestic violence report. You'll find out who all reads these reports. You'll find out how the domestic violence report is different from other types of reports. You'll learn how to clearly describe evidence of domestic violence and get a better understanding of the domestic violence report format.

Remember, you are the only official person from the criminal justice system who gets a firsthand sense of the case—you hear, smell, and sense what everyone else reads about. Your report must be complete. Your readers are not psychics—they will never know what information you have left out. You must develop this attitude: If it is not in the report **it did not happen.** Consider the questions **who, what, where, when, how,** and **why**—even if all those answers are not yet available.

The quality of your report can affect the success of an investigation. It can determine whether a prosecuting attorney charges the case, and it can affect your credibility when you testify in court.

Ready to go? Follow the training and you'll be on your way to writing outstanding reports and increasing convictions.

Overview

"The Call"

Directions:

- **Read** the dispatch information below.
- **Watch** the video *"The Call."*
- **Take notes** on pages 6-7 as you watch.
- **Write a report narrative** on pages 8-9.

Be thorough. You will refer to this report a number of times as you go through the training. Write the report as you normally would in your usual style. We'll be making changes and fine-tuning it as we go through the training.

Dispatch Information:

- Time: 1800 Hours
- Arrival: 1804 hours
- Address: 4932 Park Street
- Neighbor said:
  "We heard a female screaming and yelling."
- Wife: Maryann McCarthy   DOB 4/17/78
- Husband: Frank McCarthy   DOB 6/7/75
- Son: Timothy   DOB 3/04/08

"The Call"

LERC *Report Writing*

"The Call"

Notes:

"The Call"

Notes:

"The Call"

"THE CALL" INCIDENT REPORT
Directions: Write your Report Narrative below:

"The Call"

Notes:

CHAPTER 1
Everyday Language

> **OBJECTIVES**
>
> ▶ Use short everyday words.
> ▶ Write short sentences.
> ▶ Identify people by name, and make sure pronoun references are clear.
> ▶ Eliminate police jargon and "codes."

Use short, everyday words.
Some officers resist this because they equate simple words with simple-mindedness. Some officers also think that using official-sounding words makes them sound more credible.

One of Winston Churchill's famous sayings about writing:
"Small men use large words;
Large men use small words."

Write short sentences.
An easy way to write short sentences is to limit each sentence to just one idea. It can be difficult to read a report quickly when you have to slog through long, run-on sentences. The use of short sentences actually can increase the amount of information in your report.

Identify people by name, and make sure pronoun references are clear.
Make sure the person or thing being referred to by "he," "she," or "it" is obvious. You don't want the reader to have to re-read parts of the report to figure out what or whom you are referring to.

Eliminate police jargon and "codes."
Anticipate that your report will be read by people outside of your agency. They may not understand the "police-like" abbreviations, acronyms, or codes we often use in our reports.

Short Everyday Words

▸ A. Use Short Everyday Words

Write your reports using plain English. Simple words in simple sentences work best. In law enforcement we have a tendency to use official-sounding terminology rather than plain, everyday language.

Unnecessarily wordy:
The complainant advised this reporting officer that an altercation had occurred between the two tenants.

This example is less wordy, but could be better:
Smith related to me that Jones and Miller had been fighting.

Simple but more accurate:
Smith told me Jones grabbed Miller by the shirt and pushed him down.

Writing sentences with short, everyday words is a characteristic of professional writing. A simple sentence is the strongest statement an officer can write.

1 Everyday Language

Short Everyday Words

The male subject exited the vehicle and proceeded to initiate an altercation. Huh?

Ironically, we often choose an "official word" which is actually less precise than a simpler word. When you write "transported" you may mean "driven," "carried," "flown," etc. Say what you mean.

Some overused and troublesome words have a special appeal to police officers. Certain words just sound like they should be in a police report. One of these overused words is *"indicate."*

Weaver indicated where he had hidden the gun.

A person can "indicate" by speaking, nodding his head, pointing, or by using other nonverbal means. Here's a better way to write it:

Weaver pointed and said, "The gun is in the trash can."

Other troublesome words are *"proceeded"* and *"observed."* They may sound official, but a shorter, simpler word would give clearer meaning.

"Official": *I observed Williams throw a plastic baggie out the window.*

Simple: *I saw Williams throw a plastic baggie out the window.*

LERC Report Writing

Write Short Sentences

EXERCISE 1

Directions: Substitute a simpler word for each of the following words. (There may be more than one right answer.)

Example:
Informed   _____Told_____

1. Observed   _____Saw_____
2. Commenced   _____
3. Documented   _____
4. Multitude   _____
5. Related   __Told or said__
6. Utilized   _____
7. Ascertained   ____learned____
8. In reference to _____

EXERCISE 2

Directions: In each sentence, substitute a simpler word for the word in parentheses.

Example: At 2015 she was (*transported*) ___driven___ back to her apartment.

1. Officer Able (*detected*) ___smelled___ the odor of alcohol on the man.

2. They told me that they had left the residence at (*approximately*) ___about___ 2200 hours.

3. Officer Able (*exited*) ___got out___ his squad car.

4. (*Due to the fact*) ___because___ the victim dropped the assault charges, we (*ceased*) ___stopped___ the investigation.

5. When I found the lost child I quickly (*notified*) ___called___ the parents.

6. During the stakeout, we (*utilized*) ___used___ the new night vision system.

For exercise answers see page 122

14

1 Everyday Language

▶ B. Write Short Sentences

Writing a clear and concise report requires more than just using simple words. It also requires writing short sentences. Simplify your writing. Omit needless words. Place only one idea in each sentence.

Complex: *It should be noted that I had seen Jenkins driving the same car two weeks ago.*

Simple: *I saw Jenkins driving the same car two weeks ago.*

Look at the following run-on sentence from an actual police report:

```
The residents stated their concerns of the aggressive
dog being allowed to stay in the area due to them
having small children who play outside and after
seeing how the dog became very aggressive toward
officers and other persons.
```

This sentence should be broken into several shorter sentences. Let's break it down.

The residents told the officer several things:

- They were worried about the aggressive dog staying in the area.
- Their small children play outside.
- They saw the dog get aggressive toward the officers and other people.

Take a look at a rewrite of the above sentence. Breaking one long, run-on sentence into three short sentences gave the report more clarity:

```
The residents told me they had concerns about
allowing the aggressive dog to stay in the area.
They were worried because they have small children
who play outside.  They were also alarmed by the
dog's aggressiveness toward other people and us.
```

Write Short Sentences

LERC *Report Writing*

EXERCISE 3

Directions: Read through the following sentences. Rewrite each one. Break it into as many separate sentences as necessary. Express one idea per sentence. (Watch for the "ands" and "buts.") Omit needless words.

Example: I smelled alcohol on his breath and he did state that he had been drinking beer, after which I did ask him to submit to standardized field sobriety tests to determine if he was under the influence of alcohol.

Write Short Sentences

I smelled alcohol on his breath. He said he had been drinking beer. I asked him to submit to standardized field sobriety tests to determine if he was under the influence of alcohol.

1. Officer Chandler and I arrived at 1500 York Avenue at 0644 and knocked on the front door and because the door was open and there was crying coming from the back of the house we went into the house to investigate.

   Officer Chandler and I arrived at 1500 York avenue at 0644. We knocked on the front door. The door was open. There was crying from the back of the house, so we went in to investigate.

2. The driver attempted to stop her car at the intersection of 33rd and Drew Street, but the road surface was icy and she was driving over the speed limit and she ended up nearly hitting a pedestrian and sliding through a red traffic light.

   The driver attempted to stop her car at the intersection of 33rd and drew street. The road surface was icy. She was driving over the speed limit. She nearly hit a pedestrian. She slid through a red light.

3. Due to the fact that the suspect James Rockhold verbally confessed to me that he hit his wife, and because I observed injuries in the way of bruises and scratches on her face, I arrested Mr. Rockhold for assaulting his wife.

   James Rockhold told me he hit his wife. I saw bruises and scratches on her face. I arrested Mr. Rockhold for assault.

For exercise answers see page 122

1 Everyday Language

Omit needless words.
Below is a portion of an actual report written by a police officer.

> Saturday, December 9, 2016, while on patrol in the 500 block of Bonner Street, I, Officer MARTY EDWARDS, observed a red Honda Civic Si 2-dr CA 485VCT parked near the swimming pool at the City Park. I observed the engine was not running at this time. Upon further investigation, I observed a white male subject sitting in the front passenger seat of the vehicle. I recognized the subject as SAMUEL HOLT. The subject did not respond to me when I knocked on the door and window of the vehicle. During this time OFFICER MIRANDA arrived at the location to assist me. At this time I opened the door of the vehicle to check the welfare of HOLT. HOLT looked at me and then closed his eyes. I then called his name several times and finally he awoke. I noticed that his eyes were bloodshot and he was unable to unzip his coat to remove his hands from inside. OFFICER MIRANDA assisted HOLT with his coat and then he was asked to step out of the vehicle. HOLT had trouble getting out of his car and his speech was very slurred. At this time I decided Holt was under the influence of some substance causing his intoxicated state.

Write Short Sentences

Many needless words can be eliminated without altering the substance of the report. Read the report again, skipping the deleted words.

> Saturday, December 9, 2016, while on patrol in the 500 block of Bonner Street, I, Officer Marty Edwards, observed a red Honda Civic Si 2-dr CA 485VCT parked near the swimming pool at the City Park. ~~I observed~~ The engine was not running. ~~at this time.~~ ~~Upon further investigation, I observed~~ A white male ~~subject~~ was sitting in the front passenger seat. ~~of the vehicle.~~ I recognized the man ~~subject~~ as Samuel Holt. ~~The subject~~ Holt did not respond ~~to me~~ when I knocked on the door and window. ~~of the vehicle.~~ ~~During this time~~ Officer Miranda arrived ~~at the location~~ to assist me. ~~At this time~~ I opened the door of the vehicle to check ~~the~~ Holt's welfare. ~~of Holt.~~ Holt looked at me and ~~then~~ closed his eyes. I ~~then~~ called his name several times and finally he awoke. ~~I noticed that~~ His eyes were bloodshot and he was unable to unzip his coat to remove his hands from inside. Officer Miranda assisted Holt with his coat and ~~then~~ he was asked to step out of the vehicle. Holt had trouble getting out of his car and his speech was very slurred. ~~At this time~~ I decided Holt was under the influence of some substance causing his intoxicated state.

Write Short Sentences

This segment of the report was originally **206** words. Forty words (**19%!**) were eliminated. Even more could be removed by rewriting or reorganizing the narrative.

Does the removal of the words change the presentation of the facts? No. The facts are the same, but the revision presents them in a concise way—a neater package if you will.

Another consideration is the need to justify the contact and subsequent detention of Mr. Holt. Establishing reasonable suspicion and probable cause is a critical part of the report. These issues will be dealt with in **Chapter 5, Legal Requirements**.

Look at the deleted words that were removed.

WAIT! Let's eliminate some words from that sentence:

Look at the deleted words ~~that were removed~~:

I observed and *I noticed that*
When a report has placed you at the scene, it is usually not necessary to precede your observations with *I observed* or *I noticed*. It is assumed any observations described are your own. Only when other officers see something you do not should you identify who made the observation.

at this time
When a report is written in chronological order, *at this time* and similar phrases are unnecessary.

upon further investigation
Keep it simple. Just tell what happened next and these words can be omitted.

subject
This is one of the most overused words in police reports. Imagine a report with *the male subject* and *the female subject*. What's wrong with *man* and *woman*? Don't write three words when one will do.

that
Nine times out of ten the word *that* can be eliminated.

Duncan said that he would show me where he hid the gun.
Duncan said he would show me where he hid the gun.

the welfare of Holt
Holt's welfare is simpler and sounds better.

1 Everyday Language

CHECK YOUR OWN WRITING

Directions: Look over the incident report you wrote at the beginning of the training ("The Call," pages 8-9). Check it for simple words and short sentences:

Simple words
Can you find any long "official sounding" words in your report? Substitute simple informal words below:

"OFFICIAL"	SIMPLE

Check Your Own Writing

TIP: Look in the **EXTRAS** section (page 130) for a list of simple words. Use them to replace "official" words and lengthy phrases.

Short Sentences
How many sentences could you have shortened? _____

Strike out any unnecessary words.
How many did you delete? _____

19

C. Identify People by Name, and Make Sure Pronoun References are Clear

Pronoun References

Use names when available rather than referring to people as "suspect," "complainant," and "victim." Drop titles like "Mr." when possible.

Unclear: *The witness told this officer the suspect hit the victim with a leaf rake.*
Clear: *Sizemore told me Mullins hit Colvin with a leaf rake.*

Establish name references when using pronouns such as "he," "she," and "it."
Make sure the person or thing referred to by *he, she,* or *it* is obvious. The reader should not have to re-read parts of the report to understand whom or what these pronouns represent.

Example: *When I arrived, I saw Smith in the middle of the field by a large backhoe. He was arguing with Johnson.*

Clearly, the only thing "he" can refer to is Smith.

Example: *I approached the house and noticed a dog on the porch. It fit the description given by dispatch.*

In this example the reader doesn't know if "it" refers to the dog, the porch, or the house. This is clearer:

Rewrite: *I approached the house and saw a dog on the porch. The dog fit the description given by dispatch.*

Low hanging wires are hazardous to pedestrians. You must eliminate them immediately... Huh???

1 Everyday Language

EXERCISE 4:

Directions: In the following sentences what *it*, *his*, and *her* refer to is unclear. Rewrite them in any way you wish to make them clear. (There may be more than one correct answer.)

Example: The cat had bitten the daughter twice before. The family was making plans to get rid of her.

The cat had bitten the daughter twice before. The family was making plans to get rid of the daughter. Just kidding! The cat! The cat!

Pronoun References

1. I found a jogging suit, duct tape and a pocketknife inside the trunk of the yellow Ford Mustang. I put it in a sealed bag for evidence.

2. I asked the passenger to wait in the car and I talked to Jim Fletch about his behavior.

3. I saw Amy Johnson in the parking lot holding a knife and Jane Bakke mumbling and shuffling slowly in circles. I tried talking to her and did not get a response.

For exercise answers see page 123

LERC Report Writing

Make sure the reader knows who you are talking about. This lack of clear detail is exactly what defense attorneys love to pick apart.

When writing about people who have the same last name, make sure to differentiate between each person. This can be especially confusing during domestics or child abuse cases where you may talk to several family members.

Eliminate Police Jargon & "Codes"

> **D. Eliminate Police Jargon and "Codes."**

Don't write sentences like *"786 responded to a B&E."* Prosecutors, victim advocates, and others not familiar with police terminology will read your report. Use plain language that people outside your agency can understand. Write *"Officer Martin responded to a breaking and entering call."*

Avoid vague "boiler plate language" such as:
a hand-to-hand transaction
Say exactly what you saw (exchange of money, small white objects, green leafy substance, plastic baggie, hand cupped as if the suspect were trying to hide something, etc.) You are articulating the legal reason for further action.

furtive gestures
Describe the conduct, e.g., reaching over, looking over his shoulder, quick turnaround, bending over for a brief moment, reaching under his seat, etc. The term "furtive gestures" describes many different behaviors and actions. Be specific and detailed. Remember, you are articulating the legal reason for a frisk or protective weapons sweep.

frisk for officer safety
State the specific facts or reasons you are concerned for your safety, e.g., the suspect clenched his hands into fists; the suspect was yelling; you saw a bulge in his waistband; you have known the suspect to be armed in the past; you were investigating a robbery, etc. Remember, you are articulating the legal reason for conducting a frisk.

1 Everyday Language

CHECK YOUR OWN WRITING

Directions: Look over the incident report you wrote at the beginning of the training ("The Call," pages 8-9). Check it for:

Unclear pronoun references
How many times did you use a pronoun without clear reference to who was doing the action? ____

Police jargon and "codes"
Did you use any police terminology that could be confusing to someone outside your agency?   Yes ____
                                                             No ____

Check Your Own Writing

Notes:

2 Writing Tips

CHAPTER 2
Writing Tips

> **OBJECTIVES**
>
> ▶ Use "I" or "me" to refer to yourself.
> ▶ Avoid the incorrect use of "myself."
> ▶ Never use "I seen," "I been," "I says," or "I go."
> ▶ Write in the past tense.
> ▶ Use "did" sparingly in your reports.
> ▶ Use the active voice.

You put a great deal of effort into your calls for service. A well-written report reinforces that effort; a shoddy report destroys it. A report should "paint a picture" of the incident. You want your supervisors, the prosecutor, and others to envision the same things you did. Here are some writing tips to help paint a clearer picture.

Use "I" or "me" to refer to yourself.
Once you have stated your name in a report, use "I" or "me" instead of writing "this officer" when referring to yourself. Using "I" is natural. The use of "I" simplifies your report and eliminates awkward writing:

Incorrect: *This officer interviewed Craig Miller.*

Correct: *I interviewed Craig Miller.*

Avoid the incorrect use of "myself."
The word "myself" is often used incorrectly. Generally, the correct word to use is "I" or "me."

Incorrect: *Officer Rogde and myself approached the car.*

Correct: *Officer Rogde and I approached the car.*

LERC Report Writing

Writing Tips Objectives

Never use "I seen," "I been," "I says," or "I go."
These are grammatically incorrect.

Incorrect: *We seen him get into the van.*
Correct: *We saw him get into the van.*

Write in the past tense.
Even if you are a witness to a crime in progress, everything you see, do, and hear will be written into your report as an event that occurred in the past. Obviously the report is written after the event.

Incorrect: *I listen at the door before I knock.*
Correct: *I listened at the door before I knocked.*

Use "did" sparingly in your reports.
This is one of the most overused and needless words found in police reports. Take it out whenever possible.

Avoid: *did say, did see, did handcuff.*
Use: *I said, I saw, I handcuffed.*

Use the active voice.
The *voice* of a verb tells whether its subject performs an act (active), or is acted upon (passive).

Active: *The man grabbed the boy.*
Passive: *The boy was grabbed by the man.*

Tell the reader who did the action. Knowing who did the action or made the statement is crucial to the investigator or prosecutor.

Use "I" or "Me" to Refer to Yourself

A. Use "I" or "Me" to Refer to Yourself

Most agencies prefer reports written in "first person." That means you refer to yourself as "I" once you have stated your name. Some departments prefer "third person" reports. In a third person report, you would refer to yourself by using your name rather than "I," "this officer," or "reporting officer." Third person is preferred by some agencies with complex computerized report forms where there might be some confusion about who "I" is. Case reports or summaries of an investigation are often written in third person because they are usually a compilation of the work of several officers.

2 Writing Tips

EXERCISE 1

Directions: Mark the sentences which correctly use "I" or "me."

☐ Officer John Oates and I went to 5018 Oliver Street to interview the suspect.

☐ At the accident scene I found the driver needed a sign language interpreter.

☐ I, Officer Marks, stopped Jim January for speeding.

For exercise answers see page 124

Avoid the Incorrect Use of "Myself"

▶ B. Avoid the Incorrect Use of "Myself"

The word *myself* is often used incorrectly. It can only be used correctly if the word *I* is the subject of the sentence. A good example is, "*I bought myself a new car,*" or "*I will do it myself.*"

EXERCISE 2

Directions: Replace the word *myself* with the correct pronoun.

Example: Suspect Jones tried to escape from Sergeant Brown and *(myself)* __me__.

1. Officer Winston and *(myself)* __I__ were the first officers to arrive on the scene.

2. Her injury was not visible to *(myself)* __me__ during the initial investigation.

3. Deane handed the car keys and wallet to *(myself)* __me__.

4. Officer Mader and *(myself)* __I__ handcuffed Ralph Kubers.

For exercise answers see page 124

LERC Report Writing

> **C. Never Use "I Seen," "I Been," "I Says," or "I Go"**

These are grammatically incorrect. Instead, use "*I saw,*" "*I was,*" or "*I said.*"

EXERCISE 3

Directions: Rewrite the following sentences with the correct verb form.

Example: I seen a white male run out of the store.
I saw a white male run out of the store.

Never Use "I Seen…"

1. I been out there twice to look for evidence. *(was)*
   ~~I was out there twice to look for evidence~~

2. She been going to that club every weekend for two years. *(was)* *(weak)*

3. He ~~goes~~, "Keep your hands off me!"
   said

4. I ~~seen~~ her crying, but she ~~goes~~ "I'm fine, thank you."
   saw   said

5. I ~~says~~ to her, "Ma'am, I need to see your driver's license."
   said

For exercise answers see page 124

CHECK YOUR OWN WRITING

Directions: Look over the incident report you wrote at the beginning of the training ("The Call," pages 8-9). Check it for:

Use of "I" or "me"
How many times did you use "this officer" or "this writer" instead of "I" or "me"? _____

Incorrect use of "myself"
How many times was "myself" used incorrectly? _____

Use of "I seen," "I been," "I says," or "I go"
How many times were these (or any other obvious grammatical errors) made? _____

Check Your Own Writing

Write in the Past Tense

> ▶ **D. Write in the Past Tense**

Verb tenses describe whether the action is in the past, present, or future. In most incident reports you will use past tense verbs. These words show that the events have already occurred.

Examples of past tense verbs: Ran, handcuffed, booked, told, drove.

EXERCISE 4

Directions: Fill in the blank with the past tense verb.

Example: I *(tell)* __told__ the man that he could not rake his leaves into the street.

1. When the suspect was found he *(confess)* __confessed__ to setting the fire.

2. Jon Doe *(says)* __said__ he left the two year old in the car because the child was screaming.

3. Two neighborhood kids *(take)* __took__ rocks and *(break)* __broke__ the windows.

4. John Hanson *(calls)* __called__ me back with the serial number of his stolen pistol.

For exercise answers see page 124

2 Writing Tips

▶ E. Use "Did" Sparingly in Your Reports

Cut this overused word out of reports whenever possible.

Avoid: *did say, did see, did handcuff.*
Use: *I said, I saw, I handcuffed.*

You may use "did" for emphasis, but only very rarely.

Acceptable: *He said he had tried to crawl up the embankment to the road, and the grass there did look flattened.*

Incorrect: *I did respond to the call at 0300 hours.*
Correct: *I responded to the call at 0300 hours.*

EXERCISE 5

Directions: Rewrite the following sentences in the past tense without using *did*.

Example: The car *(did cross)* _crossed_ the center line.

At the beginning of the interview Andrews *(did turn)* _turned_ off the stereo.

Miller told me that Cleary *(did call)* _called_ him at 0840 hours.

Jones *(did say)* _said_ that Davis had a "kitchen knife" in his right hand.

Use "Did" Sparingly

For exercise answers see page 124

EXERCISE 6

Directions: Rewrite the following report in the past tense and without using the emphatic verb form "did."

Use "Did" Sparingly

On 3/23/2017 at 1950 hours I did respond to a domestic at 3397 Irving Avenue North. I arrived at 2002 hours. Officer Farr also arrived at that time. We met the complainant and victim, Alisa Mathews (D.O.B. 12-01-88). She said she and her husband got into an argument, but that everything is OK. She said that he did not hit her. She said he did not even yell at her. She did try to get us to leave the house. Officer Farr and I did go and talk with James Mathews, Alisa's husband. He told us she gets hysterical if she doesn't get her way. He said she threatened to call the cops if he didn't let her keep some clothing she bought. He did say he grabbed her by the upper arms and held her back from attacking him. Alisa does not have any injuries or marks on her arms.

Use the Active Voice

For exercise answers see page 125

> **F. Use the Active Voice**

Using the active voice of verbs tells the reader who or what did the action. The passive voice is used when the subject is acted upon.

Active: *The man grabbed the boy.*
Passive: *The boy was grabbed by the man.*

In the active voice:
The "doer" comes before the verb.
Statements are direct, brief, and natural.

In the passive voice:
The subject receives the action.
Statements are less direct, longer, and harder to understand. Check out any insurance policy—the passive voice generally runs wild!

Here is the key to remember: Put the "doer" in front of the action.
Sentences in the passive voice are often vague. Knowing who did the action or made the statement is crucial to the reader of the report.

Passive: *Drugs were found in McCain's pocket.*

This sentence lacks information. We don't know who found the drugs. The prosecutor needs to know whom to call to testify about finding the drugs. This lack of information could affect the admissibility of the drugs or could impeach the credibility of the officer when testifying. **Remember that details can make or break a case.**

Active: *Officer Rikert found the drugs in McCain's pocket.*

LERC Report Writing

Use the Active Voice

EXERCISE 7

Directions: Mark these sentences as "A" active or "P" passive.

Example: _____A_____ Mark gave me the gun.

1. _____ The gun was given to me by Mark.
2. _____ The baby was handed to me.
3. _____ Sommers handed me the baby.
4. _____ The driver jumped out of the car.
5. _____ The witness was talked to by me.
6. _____ Drugs were found on the defendant.
7. _____ The car hit the barrier.
8. _____ The defendant was searched.

EXERCISE 8

Directions: Change these passive sentences to active.

Example: Williams was placed under arrest by Officer Beamer.
Officer Beamer placed Williams under arrest.

1. The driver was asked for his identification by Officer Mader.
   Officer Mader asked the driver for his identification.

2. Johnson was patted down for weapons by me.
   I patted Johnson down for weapons.

3. Peterson ~~was asked by me~~ to recite the alphabet.
   I asked

For exercise answers see page 125

34

2 Writing Tips

CHECK YOUR OWN WRITING

Directions: Look over the incident report you wrote at the beginning of the training ("The Call," pages 8-9). Check it for:

Writing in the past tense
How many sentences were not written in the past tense? _____

Unnecessary use of "did"
How many times was the word "did" used unnecessarily? _____

Use of the active voice
How many times did you use the passive voice instead of the active voice? _____

Check Your Own Writing

Notes:

3 Organization

CHAPTER 3
Organization

> **OBJECTIVES**
>
> ▶ Organize paragraphs.
> ▶ Use a forecasting sentence.
> ▶ Write in chronological order.
> ▶ Use headings when appropriate.

Organization Objectives

When you sit down to write your report, you are telling a story. All stories have structure so the reader can follow along easily. The structure is usually chronological with a beginning, a middle, and an end. The first step to organizing your story is to break it down into paragraphs.

Organize paragraphs.
Paragraphs are the basic organizational unit in any story. Each paragraph should contain a single topic.

Use a forecasting sentence.
A forecasting sentence is the first sentence of a paragraph. It tells the reader the topic of the whole paragraph. Here are some examples:

I conducted the field sobriety tests with the following results.

I photographed numerous injuries on the victim's body.

I found several pieces of evidence at the accident scene.

Write in chronological order.
Most police officers write their reports using the chronological order of events or what is sometimes called "cascading narrative." The timing of actions and events at a crime scene can be important to the case.

Use headings when appropriate.
It may be helpful to use headings to organize your report further. In addition, some officers use bullets to list information under headings. Officers can simply write a lead-in sentence like "*Jane Doe made the following statements:*" and then list each new statement with a bullet.

LERC Report Writing

A. Organize Paragraphs

Organize Paragraphs

To make your reports clearer, take a few minutes to gather your thoughts. Sort and organize those thoughts into chunks of information. It might be easiest to think in terms of who, what, and where.

The chunks of information become paragraphs in your report. Paragraphs are the basic organizational unit in any document. They represent a single topic. A police report is made up of many topics. Here are some examples:

I charged Smith with driving under the influence.
Jones gave me her statement.
I found several pieces of evidence.

Paragraphs are thought organizers. Keep in mind that a good paragraph deals with one topic and is supported by key ideas/facts, details, and examples.

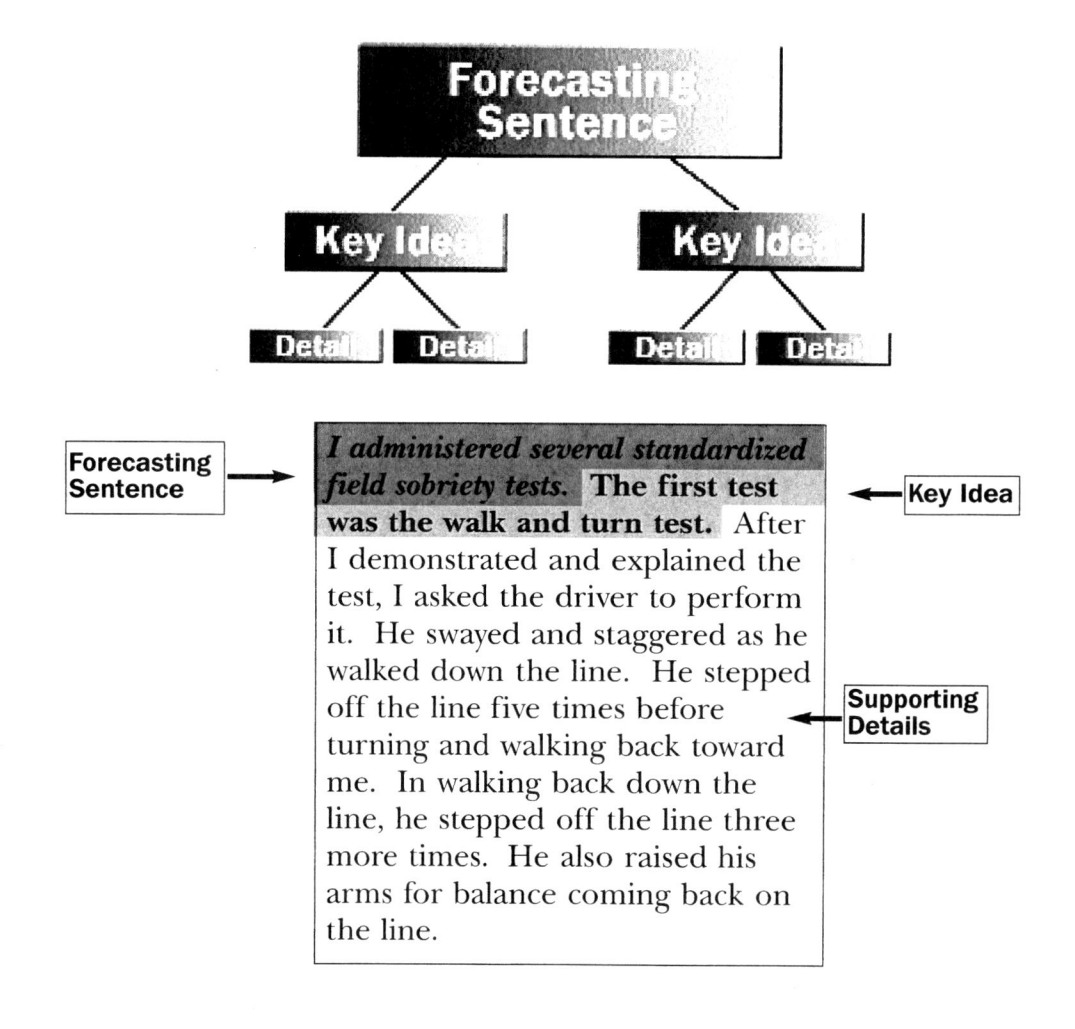

Forecasting Sentence
├── **Key Idea**
│   ├── Detail
│   └── Detail
└── **Key Idea**
    ├── Detail
    └── Detail

Forecasting Sentence → *I administered several standardized field sobriety tests.* **The first test was the walk and turn test.** ← **Key Idea** After I demonstrated and explained the test, I asked the driver to perform it. He swayed and staggered as he walked down the line. He stepped off the line five times before turning and walking back toward me. In walking back down the line, he stepped off the line three more times. He also raised his arms for balance coming back on the line. ← **Supporting Details**

38

3 Organization

▶ B. Use a Forecasting Sentence

A good paragraph expresses a single topic. That topic is broadly stated in the forecasting sentence. The forecasting sentence will be supported by any number of facts, reasons, and examples that provide the details.

Example:
Deb Jamison said her car was stolen. She gave me the following description of her vehicle. It is a navy blue 2015 Honda Accord. It is registered in Nebraska with license number JGH 534. The car has a broken left front turn signal.

Forecasting sentence:
Deb Jamison said her car was stolen.

Key idea:
She gave me a description of her car.

Three supporting details:
- It is a navy blue 2015 Honda Accord.
- It is registered in Nebraska with license number JGH 534
- The car has a broken left front turn signal.

And I thought "It's going to rain tomorrow" was a forecasting sentence!

LERC Report Writing

Use a Forecasting Sentence

EXERCISE 1

Directions: Find the sentence in each group that is the best forecasting sentence for the paragraph as a whole and circle it.

TIP: Which sentence contains a topic so big (or so general) that all the others help to explain it?

Group I

a) It reduces an officer's reaction time, thereby giving him or her a better chance to survive.

b) There are several reasons police agencies should strive for realistic firearms training.

c) There is a reduced civil liability. The agency can show that the officer has been trained under "real life" conditions.

Group II

a) The responding officer must evaluate the situation properly and take appropriate action.

b) Arrests can't be made if the officer doesn't know a crime has occurred.

c) Confessions from suspects must be obtained in a way that ensures the statement's admissibility in court.

d) Knowledge of the law is important for a police officer to perform effectively.

e) This is important because officers can be sued for false arrest.

For exercise answers see page 126

3 Organization

▶ C. Write in Chronological Order

An easy way to organize your report is to describe things in the order they happened. Your report will make more sense to the reader if they can follow you through time.

When you use a chronological format to write your reports, transition words such as *first*, *next*, and *finally* can be helpful. Transitions help the reader locate where they are in the chronology of the incident.

Example:

First, we examined the door...

Next, we placed the evidence in bags...

Finally, we gave Mr. Melone a Victim's Rights card...

▶ D. Use Headings When Appropriate

Another way to create organization in your report is to use headings. Headings allow you to sort and categorize facts that belong together. They help both the writer and the reader. The writer can easily sort the information, yet still write in a chronological sequence. The reader can easily pick out details while skimming the document.

A worksheet with headings may be useful in taking notes in the field. Good notes will make your reports easier to write.

On the following page is a suggested model of headings that can be used to help organize a report. (Your department may have its own format for specific types of reports.)

Write in Chronological Order

Use Headings When Appropriate

HEADINGS:

Preliminary Information

Officer's Observations and Actions

Victim's/Complainant's Statements

Witness's Statements

Suspect's Statements

Investigation of the Scene

Evidence Collected

Disposition

Preliminary Information
The preliminary information paragraph tells how you got involved in the incident.
    Key Points:
- Date, time, location (when and where).
- Type of incident (who and what).
- Source of call, e.g., radio call, citizen's call, informant, crime report, assisting agency, observation, etc. (how).

Officer's Observations/Actions
Specify what you did and why.
    Key Points:
- Describe what you saw, did, smelled, or heard when you arrived on the scene.
- Be specific.
- Use factual statements.

3 Organization

Victim/Witness/Suspect Statements
Victim/witness/suspect statements provide an essential link in the continuity of the investigations. They can be used in guiding the investigation, as well as for court evidence. Include statements like, *"I didn't steal that much..."* or *"He owed me money..."*
> Key Point:
> - Remember to state what they told you they had seen, done, or heard. Important statements should be quoted directly using quotation marks. (We'll do this in Chapter 4.)

Investigation of the Scene
Describe the activities of any investigation following your initial observations/actions and statements. These are pertinent activities done in the pursuit of evidence.
> Key Points:
> - Describe conditions of the scene.
> - Describe any actions taken, e.g., photographs taken, fingerprints collected.
> - Describe circumstances of location of evidence.

Evidence Collected
List all evidence gathered to this point.
> Key Points:
> - List all material evidence or seized property. Arrange each item in sequence by time and date obtained. Identify the person responsible for collecting the item and its location when collected. Document chain of custody.
> - List documents such as search warrants, arrest warrants, affidavits, subpoenas, judicial transcripts, court orders, evidence/property receipts, crime lab reports, photographs, etc.

Disposition
Identify the particulars of the arrest or the result of the incident.
> Key Points:
> - List the location of the suspect, along with any charges.
> - If the incident is a crime against property, include the recovery of any property.
> - Identify any follow-up activities.

Use Headings When Appropriate

EXERCISE 2

Directions: The following report is written in chronological order. Read it over and decide how it should be divided into paragraphs. Feel free to use headings. Put a "P" where the paragraph breaks should be

Use Headings When Appropriate

I was dispatched to 1234 Mulberry Street at 1500 hours on April 10, 2016, regarding a house burglary. When I got to the house, I met the owner, Patricia Olson. She was standing by the front door. The door was hanging by one hinge and the door frame was splintered. The deadbolt was still in the locked position. Olson said that she came home after work at about 1430 hours. She did not go into the house when she saw the front door was broken in. She said she went to a neighbor's house to call 911. Olson said her son and husband are out of town on a fishing trip. I went into the house with my pistol drawn and made a sweep to determine if the person was still inside. I saw two wet, muddy shoe prints on the floor just inside the front door. I saw the back door was open. In the study, I found the top desk drawer open and several pieces of paper lying on the floor. I called for the evidence technician, John Mikkal, and secured the scene until he arrived. Olson looked through her things and found that an envelope with about $1600 in cash was missing from the desk. I asked her if she knew who might have taken the cash. She said she had no idea. Jane Jenson, 1238 Mulberry Street, telephone (555) 234-2349, came up to me at the scene and said she had been home all day. At about 1330 hours she saw a male run from the direction of the Olson house toward the east. She recognized him as Peter Cromley, a friend of the Olson's sixteen-year-old son. Jenson said Cromley lives at 345 2nd Avenue. Officer Mikkal, the evidence technician, dusted for prints on both the front and back doors and the desk area. No fingerprints were found. He photographed the front door and the shoe prints inside the front door. I provided Olson with a case number and a Victim's Rights card. I drove to the Cromley house at 345 2nd Avenue to talk to the suspect. I knocked on the door but no one answered.

For exercise answers see next page

Here is the same report using headings:

Preliminary Information
I was dispatched to 1234 Mulberry Street at 1500 hours on April 10, 2016, regarding a house burglary.

Officer's Observations/Actions
When I got to the house, I met the owner, Patricia Olson. She was standing by the front door. The door was hanging by one hinge and the door frame was splintered. The deadbolt was still in the locked position.

Victim's Statement
Olson said that she came home after work at about 1430 hours. She did not go into the house when she saw the front door was broken in. She said she went to a neighbor's house to call 911. Olson said her son and husband are out of town on a fishing trip.

Officer's Observations/Actions
I went into the house with my pistol drawn and made a sweep to determine if the person was still inside. I saw two wet, muddy shoe prints on the floor just inside the front door. I saw the back door was open.

In the study, I found the top desk drawer open and several pieces of paper lying on the floor. I called for the evidence technician, John Mikkal, and secured the scene until he arrived.

Victim's Statement
Olson looked through her things and found that an envelope with about $1600 in cash was missing from the desk. I asked her if she knew who might have taken the cash. She said she had no idea.

Witness's Statement
Jane Jenson, 1238 Mulberry Street, telephone (555) 234-2349, came up to me at the scene and said she had been home all day. At about 1330 hours she saw a male run from the direction of the Olson house toward the east. She recognized him as Peter Cromley, a friend of the Olson's sixteen-year-old son. Jenson said Cromley lives at 345 2nd Avenue.

Investigation of the Scene
Officer Mikkal, the evidence technician, dusted for prints on both the front and back doors and the desk area. No fingerprints were found. He photographed the front door and the shoe prints inside the front door.

Disposition
I provided Olson with a case number and a Victim's Rights card. I drove to the Cromley house at 345 2nd Avenue to talk to the suspect. I knocked on the door but no one answered.

Use Headings When Appropriate

Use Headings When Appropriate

A well-organized report helps your case.
Paragraphs and headings are used to help officers organize their reports. The reader can find statements, evidence, or witness information quickly and easily. Use this format to help you include all details, facts, and statements.

A well-written report will help you quickly find facts when you testify in court. If you try to testify to something you didn't include in your report, the defense attorney will attack. It will be implied that you didn't include it in your report because it never happened and that you are simply making it up. Your credibility with the jury will be lost. It is important to write a **complete** report and never leave out details which could be important at trial.

Conclusion
It takes only a few minutes to turn a mediocre report into an exceptional one. Good reports allow prosecutors to charge more cases, negotiate for better pleas, and ultimately get more convictions. Sloppy reports undermine the hard work you do handling your calls. Take the extra time to do the job right.

3 Organization

CHECK YOUR OWN WRITING

Directions: Look over the incident report you wrote at the beginning of the training ("The Call," pages 8-9). Check it for:

Paragraphs
Did each paragraph include only one main topic?   YES ____
                                                  NO ____

Forecasting sentences
Did you write sentences which forecast what the
paragraph was about?   YES ____
                                                  NO ____

Chronological order
Is your report written in chronological order?   YES ____
                                                  NO ____

Headings
Did you use headings when appropriate?   YES ____
                                                  NO ____

Check Your Own Writing

Notes:

CHAPTER 4
Facts & Details

> **OBJECTIVES**

- Use specific language instead of general language.
- Attribute testimony or statements to a person.
- Stick to the facts...
- ...and include all the facts.
- Don't jump to conclusions.

Use specific language instead of general language.
Say exactly what you mean. Your goal is to paint a picture for the reader of everything you saw, heard, and did.

Attribute testimony or statements to a person.
If it is not clear who did or said what, it is difficult to bring a witness forward to testify in a court case.

Stick to the facts...
Making factual statements is one of the most important principles to follow in law enforcement writing. Nothing can discredit a report more than the presence of opinion, conjecture, or unsubstantiated conclusions.

...and include all the facts.
Part of your job is knowing things. You should have extensive knowledge about the area where you work—you know the "usual suspects," what methods the bad guys are using, and where the "hot spots" are located. You enter situations with a great deal of information the readers of your reports do not possess. It is equally important that you assume the reader of your report knows nothing about your case. If you want the reader to know it, put it in the report.

Don't jump to conclusions.
The facts should speak for themselves. Without facts there is no case.

Facts & Details Objectives

LERC Report Writing

In the first three chapters, you learned skills which will make your reports clearer and easier to read. But frankly, a report which has misspellings and bad grammar but shows off good police work and reporting will still get a conviction. Now we are entering the meat of this training—providing you with the skills to make your reports stand up in court and increase convictions.

Use Specific Language Instead of General Language

A. Use Specific Language Instead of General Language

Paint a picture for your reader.
You are usually the only person in the entire legal system with access to the scene. You know what you saw, heard, and smelled. No one else who reads your report will know any of these facts unless you put them in your report. When you use specific terms, it is easier for your reader to visualize the scene as you did.

Example: The bedroom door was hanging by one hinge; dresser drawers were overturned on the carpet. The bed frame had been broken and the headboard was splintered. The bedcovers were wet and smelled of alcohol. The glass in the window was broken. Women's clothing and broken glass were on the ground outside the window. The phone had been ripped from the wall; the wall jack was broken and the phone was in pieces on the floor. There was a black extension cord on the floor in the middle of the room. Two children, ages 3 and 5, were huddled together in the closet; both were shaking and crying. I smelled urine in the corner where they were huddled.

4 Facts & Details

The more general a term is, the more meanings it can have. The more meanings it has, the more confusing it can become. Vague and confusing details open a report up to criticism. The more specific your language, the more likely your reader will picture the same things you did.

Words have different meanings for different people. The word *fighting* might mean *talking with raised voices* or *shooting at each other*. *Acting crazy* might mean *sitting still and staring* or *running down the sidewalk while taking his clothes off*.

Use specific terms to help paint your picture.

EXERCISE 1

Directions: Mark the following either "G" for general or "S" for specific.

Ex. __G__ Often

1. __G__ Weapon
2. __S__ 1435 hours
3. __S__ Layer of white powder
4. __G__ Slight odor
5. __S__ Screaming and crying
6. __G__ Early morning
7. __S__ 2009 Saturn Coupe, silver
8. __S__ 500 thousand dollars
9. __S__ 3" black and blue mark
10. __G__ Medium height
11. __S__ 7-inch blade
12. __G__ Belligerent

Use Specific Language Instead of General Language

For exercise answers see page 127

LERC Report Writing

Use Specific Language Instead of General Language

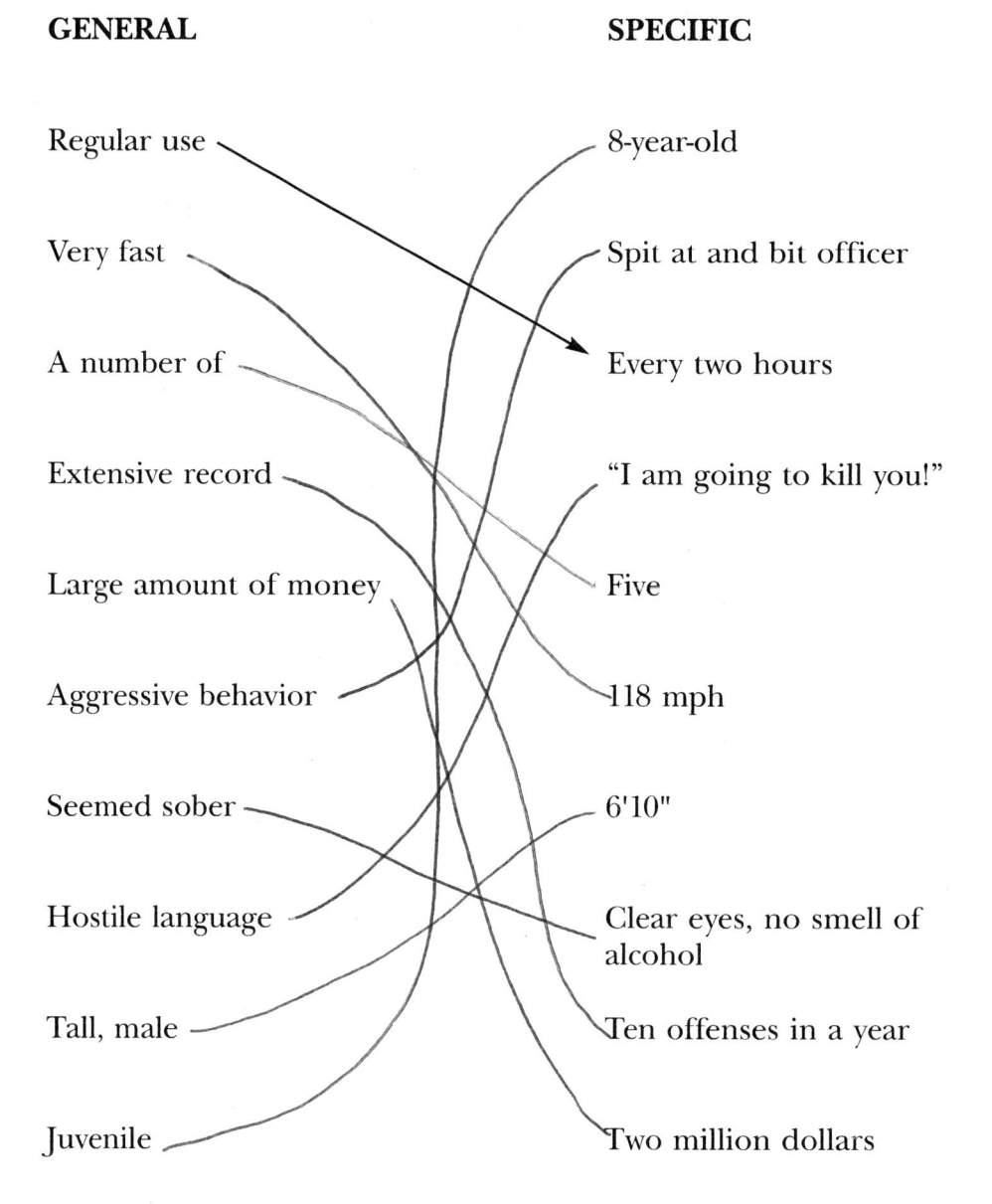

EXERCISE 2

Directions: Use lines to connect the general phrases to specific words and phrases.

GENERAL	SPECIFIC
Regular use	8-year-old
Very fast	Spit at and bit officer
A number of	Every two hours
Extensive record	"I am going to kill you!"
Large amount of money	Five
Aggressive behavior	118 mph
Seemed sober	6'10"
Hostile language	Clear eyes, no smell of alcohol
Tall, male	Ten offenses in a year
Juvenile	Two million dollars

For exercise answers see page 128

52

4 Facts & Details

▶ B. Attribute Testimony or Statements to a Person

If someone tells you something that causes action on your part, identify that person. For example, you respond to a robbery and a witness tells you the suspect is wearing a yellow football jersey. Your report should give the name and contact information of that witness.

Write important statements in quotes.
When statements are important in deciding to make an arrest or conduct a search, quote the person if you can. Incriminating statements made by a suspect should be quoted rather than summarized. Place the words within quotation marks. Quotation marks show that these are the exact words used. If you are summarizing what was said, or the exact wording is not important to the case, quotation marks are not used.

Example:
Direct quote (exact words): *Wendy Layne said, "He kicked me in the stomach."*

Quote marks not needed (summarized words): *He told me the Barracloughs were away on vacation.*

Stick to the Facts...

> ### C. Stick to the Facts

When writing the narrative section of your reports, be careful to distinguish between statements of fact and statements of opinion or conclusion.

Facts can be verified or proven:
Three people were in the vehicle.

Opinions are open to interpretation and show bias:
The victim was acting crazy!

Avoid speculation and judgments.
Be careful when you use words like *confessed* and *admitted*. These are perfectly good words to use when suspects are admitting to actual crimes, but they often appear in police reports inappropriately:

...Tucker had been playing pool with Nikiel at the time of the assault. Tucker confessed that he had 6 beers in 2 hours...

The word *confessed* implies a statement of guilt, but having 6 beers is not a crime. (This is not a DWI case.) A better way to state this might be:

Tucker said he had 6 beers in 2 hours.

Leave your opinions out of your reports. They count for nothing in court. Stick to the facts.

4 Facts & Details

EXERCISE 3

Directions: Rewrite the following sentences. Make up details that would change them from statements of opinion to statements of fact.

Example:
Opinion: The hammer was used to break the window.
A hammer was lying on the ground below the broken window.

1. The thief broke open the cash register and stole the money.

   The cash register was open and there was no money inside.

2. The suspect gained entry through the broken kitchen window.

   Glass was scattered on the floor of the kitchen. A piece of cloth was hanging on the window sill. A footprint was also on the sill.

3. Hardy acted very aggressively when I put her into the temporary holding cell.

   Hardy kicked me and tried to hit me when I...

Stick to the Facts...

For exercise answers see page 129

D. ...and Include All the Facts

When writing your reports, assume the reader knows nothing about your case. Take a look at the first lines of an actual report:

"At about 12:15 a.m., I saw a woman loitering at the intersection of Second Avenue and Oakview Road. When I walked by, she turned her head abruptly so I could not see her face. I approached her, stopped her..."

The officer continues his report by explaining that he stopped her, and asked for consent to search her. The officer found crack cocaine in her pocket.

Unfortunately, when the prosecutor read the report, she decided there was insufficient reason to justify the stop. Without a lawful stop, the officer's actions, including requesting consent to search, and discovery of the drugs, were impermissible.

When the officer met with the prosecutor to discuss the reasons the case wasn't charged, the officer gave the prosecutor a lot more information regarding the stop.

4 Facts & Details

What did the officer know?

- The location, Second and Oakview, was an intersection where numerous drug and prostitution arrests had been made in the past.

- The prostitutes and drug dealers usually worked the area after midnight.

- They would cross back and forth across the street to be in different jurisdictions.

- He saw her talk to the lone male occupants of two cars that pulled up to the curb. The conversations were less than one minute.

The officer thought anyone who read the first two lines of the report would understand the situation, so he left out many details of the stop. Though he had reasonable and articulable suspicion for the stop, the problem with this report stemmed from the officer's failure to tell **everything** he knew. The police work was excellent; the report was a failure.

...and Include All the Facts

57

...and Include All the Facts

Important Terms:

Reasonable and articulable suspicion
The term *articulable* is important. If something is articulable, it means you can say it or write it in a clear and effective way. Think of it as "list-able."

Statements like "I knew something was fishy" or "he was acting suspiciously" mean nothing in court. However, most officers, when pressed, can readily list (or articulate) the specific things they saw or heard which totalled up to "fishy" or "suspicious."

Probable cause and the totality of circumstances
Probable cause is defined as "a belief, based upon an officer's reasonable and prudent consideration of the totality of circumstances that a crime occurred and the subject to be arrested committed the crime."

— Draper v. United States, 338 US 307, 313 (1957)

The totality of circumstances refers to all the information and evidence available to you including, but not limited to:

- information from 911 dispatchers
- statements of all parties
- your observations
- physical evidence
- the demeanor and emotional state of all parties
- your prudent and cautious judgment of the credibility of statements
- reliable information about past incidents involving a suspect

It is not enough to follow legal procedure in making your stops and arrests. You must also document those steps in your report. Again, if it's not in your report **it did not happen.** Never assume that your reader knows any of the facts that you know. As you will see, the case depends on those facts.

4 Facts & Details

The Prosecutor

The prosecutor was new to the area. Unlike the police department's officers, she did not have any knowledge of the Second and Oakview location. While reading the report, she mistakenly read 12:15 a.m. to mean a quarter after noon. She concluded there was no reasonable suspicion for a stop based on the facts the officer provided in his report, thus making the stop, search, and subsequent arrest illegal.

Before you criticize prosecutors, remember this: They must make decisions about cases much the same way we must determine if there is sufficient suspicion to stop, and probable cause to arrest. For various reasons, we do not stop and arrest every suspect we could. For just as many reasons, prosecutors cannot pursue every case sent to them.

In this case, the report was the reason the case didn't get charged. The prosecutor can only pursue cases when reports thoroughly document the legal bases for stops, arrests, and searches. This is such an important part of report writing that we'll spend all of Chapter 5 on it.

Remember, the report often makes the difference. Write as if all readers will know nothing about the case. This will force you to include more facts and details. Thorough reports will lead to more charges and ultimately more convictions.

...and Include **All** the Facts

LERC Report Writing

...and Include All the Facts

Example 2
Here is another actual arrest report. Try to find the officer's "detailed observations" and "factual statements."

```
On 10-08-2015 at 2230 hours, I was conducting a routine
surveillance in the vicinity of 13th Street and Caldwell
Avenue North. I had been detailed to concentrate on this
area due to numerous complaints of loitering and narcotics
activity.

At approximately 2245 hours, I observed a white male, later
ID'd as Bart Murschel, approaching passersby and vehicles at
the intersection. Murschel then conducted what appeared to
be hand to hand transactions with the other parties,
consistent with what is observed in narcotics transactions.

I radioed this information to marked squads who stopped and
arrested Murschel. He was found in possession of several
baggies of suspected crack/cocaine. The suspected narcotics
were inventoried into evidence.
```

The county attorney felt he was unable to convict Murschel based on the information provided, and declined the case. The police sergeant was really angry (we'll leave out the specific language in this instance!) that the case was refused. He felt it was a solid case.

The problem is, there are virtually no facts in this report. Which facts support an arrest? What are the details beyond the vague "hand to hand transactions"? Which facts support probable cause for the arrest? This report raises more questions than it answers.

4 Facts & Details

Really, leave <u>nothing</u> out?

Obviously, you encounter many facts in your stops and investigations. Deciding which details to include in your report is a dicey problem. You need to realize that the prosecutor will require a higher level of proof for conviction (beyond a reasonable doubt) than you do to arrest (probable cause). You need to realize that your ultimate goal is not just to make an arrest, but to gain a conviction. Otherwise, what's the point? This would lead you to include every detail possible—but let's be reasonable here—that's not always going to happen.

You've arrested Michael Tucker for assault in a bar. There were 17 witnesses in the room. You've interviewed 5 of them and they all say about the same thing. Is it necessary to interview all 17 people and document their statements? Probably not.

You've talked to both people in a domestic argument. They both agree—Neil slapped Cindy across the face with his open hand; Cindy pulled Neil's hair. Their oldest daughter Erika, 11, has described the scene as well. Is it necessary to interview and document the responses of the two youngest siblings, age 4 and 6, for their account? Your best judgment tells you this would be traumatic and detrimental to the youngsters. That's an acceptable reason for not pursuing and including that information at that time.

Be aware, though, that a defense attorney will be looking at this report. If there are facts that you have left out of the report, be prepared to say why.

...and Include <u>All</u> the Facts

61

LERC *Report Writing*

...and Include All the Facts

EXERCISE 4

Directions: Look at the following list. Which items would most likely be inconsequential to a domestic violence report, and thus left out?

1. ____ A lamp was broken and on the floor.

2. ✓ Dirty dishes were in the sink.

3. ____ The man had scratches on his face.

4. ✓ It was raining hard.

5. ✓ The woman was wearing a T-shirt which read "Life's a Bitch and Then You Are One."

6. ✓ The woman called you a pig while you were interviewing her.

7. ✓ It was dark outside.

8. ____ The woman was crying.

(**Note:** It's important to know the purpose of your report. Facts about the weather conditions are obviously critical in traffic accident reports, but are they important here?)

For exercise answers see page 129

4 Facts & Details

CHECK YOUR OWN WRITING

Directions: Look over the incident report you wrote at the beginning of the training ("The Call," pages 8-9).

Check it for:
Specific and general language
How many times could you have substituted a specific term for a general one? ____

Testimony and Statements
Did you put direct quotes in quotation marks?

                        YES___
                        NO___

Facts and Opinions
How many sentences contained opinions rather than facts? ___

<u>All</u> the facts
Did you leave out any information you assumed the reader already knew?

                        YES___
                        NO___

Check Your Own Writing

LERC Report Writing

Don't Jump to Conclusions

▶ **E. Don't Jump to Conclusions**

Tell what you know, not what you think.

Read the following story:

Dispatch sent you to the local high school. When you arrived at 0638 hours, you discovered the glass front door had been smashed in. The inside walls of the school had been spray painted. Shelves had been overturned in the kitchen, and the refrigerators had been unplugged. There was a pile of scorched books in the library. The sprinkler system had soaked everything in the library.

The principal, Harry Johnson, met you at the school. He told you that at 1 a.m. he drove past the school. The school looked fine. A car full of kids he recognized from the local private school was spinning circles in the front parking lot. He told them to leave and they did after the kids swore at him. The teenagers drove a silver Taurus and the principal got the license plate number JKL 320. The principal said he felt those kids were up to no good.

The principal also told you he heard through the "grapevine" that a threat was made by two students. They said they were going to burn the school down. Those two students are out of school on a two-day suspension unrelated to the alleged threat. One of the suspended students drives an old delivery van.

A neighbor, Monica Neil, said she couldn't sleep, and saw a blue car squeal out of the school parking lot between 2 and 2:30 a.m.

A different neighbor, Mark Trellis, said he saw a white van leaving the school about 6 a.m.

4 Facts & Details

EXERCISE 5

Directions: After reviewing the story, mark the following statements as either "F" Fact or "C" Conclusion.

1. _F_ Someone broke the glass door of the school after 1 a.m.

2. _C_ The kids in the blue car vandalized the school.

3. _C_ The vandals drove a white van.

4. _F_ The private school kids drove a silver Taurus, license plate JKL 320.

5. _C_ The private school kids spray painted the school, then set off the sprinklers.

6. _C_ The suspended students drive a white van.

7. _C_ The suspended students tried to start a fire.

8. _F_ There was spray paint found on the walls inside the school.

9. _C_ One of the kids drove a car into the glass door.

Don't Jump to Conclusions

For exercise answers see page 129

Don't Jump to Conclusions

What Really Happened

The kids in the blue Taurus came back to the parking lot around 1:45 a.m., where they continued to spin circles. They lost control and hit the front door of the school shattering the glass. They fled the scene immediately.

A different group of kids (students at the high school) arrived at the school about 3 a.m. They noticed the glass in the front door of the school was broken. They took the opportunity to go into the school. They sprayed green and red paint on most of the walls, unplugged the refrigerators in the kitchen, pushed over some shelves, and then left.

One male student from the second group of kids came back alone to the school. Thinking they had left incriminating evidence, he tried to cover everything up by starting the school on fire. He ignited a pile of books in the library. This set off the sprinkler system. The water damaged books, shelves, carpeting, ceiling tiles and walls.

The students on suspension were not involved.

The white van seen at the school was a bakery truck delivering bread.

4 Facts & Details

Take a look at this photo.   What do you see?

Don't Jump to Conclusions

_____

_____

_____

_____

_____

Most of us would probably say we see six people waiting for the bus.

In reality, only two people are waiting for the bus. Two have just stopped to use the bench. One person is waiting for a ride. The last person is waiting for a drug deal.

It is easy to draw conclusions about what we observe. Sometimes we must draw conclusions, like when deciding to arrest a driver we think is under the influence of drugs or alcohol. But generally, stick to recording just the facts in your incident reports. Let your readers reach the same conclusions you did.

Summing It Up

SUMMING IT UP

In Chapter One, we looked at a portion of a police report. Read the report again:

> Saturday, December 9, 2015, while on patrol in the 500 block of Bonner Street, I, Officer Marty Edwards, observed a red Honda Civic Si 2 dr CA 485VCT parked near the swimming pool at the City Park. The engine was not running. A white male was sitting in the front passenger seat. I recognized the man as Samuel Holt. Holt did not respond when I knocked on the car's door and window. Officer Miranda arrived to assist me. I opened the door of the vehicle to check Holt's welfare. Holt looked at me and closed his eyes. I called his name several times and finally he awoke. His eyes were bloodshot and he was unable to unzip his coat to remove his hands from inside. Officer Miranda assisted Holt with his coat and he was asked to step out of the vehicle. Holt had trouble getting out of his car and his speech was very slurred. I decided Holt was under the influence of some substance causing his intoxicated state.

Let's examine this report to determine if it meets the objectives of this chapter:

Use specific language instead of general language.
Is a specific picture painted of Holt's appearance and demeanor? How could the officer have been more definite in the report?

unable to unzip his coat...
This is confusing for the reader. Was he sitting with his arms and hands inside the body of his jacket but not in the sleeves? Be specific.

had trouble getting out of his car...
This is very vague. Did he reach for the door but miss it? Did he lose his footing? Did he take 30 seconds to get his feet out of the car and onto the ground?

Attribute testimony or statements to a person.
The report mentions that Holt's speech was slurred, but there is no mention of anything he said. Was he asked what he was doing in the park after closing hours? What was his reply?

Stick to the facts...
Does the report seem to include all the facts up to this point? Some key facts are missing that could be decisive in a prosecutor's decision to proceed with this case.

4 Facts & Details

The missing facts:
The time was 1:30 a.m. and the park was closed. That information helps justify the investigatory contact.

The keys were in the ignition—not in his pocket or on the back seat. This will be an important fact in prosecuting for DUI/DWI.

There is no mention of any smell of alcohol, cannabis or chemicals on his breath or clothing. The only facts which support intoxication are:

- *bloodshot eyes*
- *unable to unzip coat*
- *had trouble getting out of his car*
- *speech was very slurred*

Any of these factors could be present if Holt had a medical condition or was suffering from hypothermia.

...and include all the facts.
The officer assumed everyone would know the park was closed and trespassing after hours was a criminal offense. Such assumptions are risky when someone outside the agency makes decisions based solely on what is written in the report.

Don't jump to conclusions.
The officer decided the man was intoxicated. Normally, we do not draw conclusions in reports—we let the facts speak for themselves. Sometimes, as with intoxicated persons, we must make decisions based on what we see before we can take further action. When we must draw conclusions, it is important to include all the facts supporting that conclusion. The sequence of events is also important. A defense attorney may question you on when you determined the person was intoxicated (and therefore not free to leave the scene). The facts must show the conclusion—at the time it was made—was reasonable.

Conclusion
If you don't have the facts, you don't have a case. It's as simple as that. If it happened and was important, put it in your report.

Summing It Up

Notes:

5 Legal Requirements

CHAPTER 5
Legal Requirements

> **OBJECTIVES**
>
> ▶ Understand the legal definitions of a crime.
> ▶ Understand the sequence of an arrest.
> ▶ Use a "legal checklist" when writing your report.

Understand the legal definitions of a crime.
Laws are the nuts and bolts of your job. The more you know and understand the details and boundaries of the laws, the more effective work you can do. You will have more confidence in your decision-making and prepare better cases. Knowing the law will also make your job easier to perform.

Understand the sequence of an arrest.
Each action you take during an investigation must be constitutionally permissible (legal). Think of each action as a link of a chain. If you do not perform an action legally, that action becomes the weak link and breaks the chain, ruining the chances of the case being successfully prosecuted.

Use a "legal checklist" when writing your report.
Using a checklist will ensure that your report contains all the elements necessary for successful prosecution. In many cases the police work was solid, but the report failed to contain the necessary legal elements. Your goal is a well-prepared report reflecting a legally conducted investigation.

A. Understand the Legal Definitions of a Crime.

Understand the Legal Definitions of a Crime

> **Note:** Your state's laws may differ from those mentioned in the training examples in this chapter. The concept, however, remains the same. Your reports must reflect legal actions.
>
> "Court cases and laws can vary between jurisdictions. We assume you know the laws of your jurisdiction, however the law can be confusing and it does change. It is advisable to speak to a prosecuting attorney or legal advisor regarding specific cases or when you are unclear on the law."

For each crime there are certain legal definitions that must be taken into account in making arrests and obtaining convictions.

For example, in most states a burglary is committed when two things happen: A person makes an unauthorized entry and does it with the intent to commit a crime. Finding a person trespassing is not enough to legally establish burglary. You must also show the suspect intended to commit a crime.

To do this:

Describe evidence of unauthorized entry.
Include how the home was entered and/or exited, e.g., *the back door had a splintered frame, the bedroom window was broken, a pry bar was found inside the front door.*

Describe evidence that there was intent to commit a crime.
Include specific details, e.g., *a HDT and DVR were missing from the living room, jewelry was missing from the bedroom, and $300 cash was missing from the bedroom desk. The a tablet and a laptop were sitting by the back door.* Include victim statements.

Describe any physical evidence observed.
Describe shoe imprints, fingerprints, broken glass, etc. Include eyewitness descriptions of suspects.

Describe any other knowledge of the case.
Perhaps this burglary fits the profile of previous burglaries or burglars. Once you have identified a suspect, include his criminal history (prior burglary arrests). Include Miranda warning when applicable.

5 Legal Requirements

Once the legal definition has been satisfied and an arrest has been made, build a strong case by reporting all the facts and details about your actions. If you arrested a suspect on the site, did you ask what he was doing there? Make sure to record all statements, disposition of evidence and other officers involved in the case.

EXERCISE 1

In your state, what elements are necessary to establish the crime of burglary? List them below.

how home was entered (broken window) pry bar, include details, missing cash, include victim statements. Physical evidence. prior knowledge

What are the elements necessary to establish the crime of assault?

Include specific details, eg a TV and VCR was missing from the living room, jewelry was missing from the bedroom desk. The CD player and stereo receiver were unplugged and sitting by the back door. Include victim statements

Understand the Legal Definitions of a Crime

Your answers will vary depending on you state's laws.

LERC Report Writing

Understand the Sequence of an Arrest

B. Understand the Sequence of an Arrest

The Fourth Amendment to the United States Constitution states, in part:

"The right of the people to be secure in their person, houses, papers, and effects against unreasonable searches and seizures shall not be violated..."

On the one hand, citizens have a constitutional right to be free from **unreasonable** searches and seizures. Society has a right to expect that the laws will be enforced fairly and impartially. On the other hand, the public needs to feel safe and wants the police to arrest and lock up the criminals. Police officers get their authority from the laws, cases, statutes, ordinances and specific department policies.

Police Actions Under the 4th Amendment
The Constitution prohibits only unreasonable searches and seizures. Therefore, any search and seizure that is reasonable is also lawful. Evolving case law has determined what actions are reasonable. The reasonableness of the officer's actions are determined by the totality of the circumstances that are clearly articulated in the police reports.

There is usually a logical and escalating sequence of events that occurs when you encounter citizens and are deciding what to do next. Depending on the situation, a combination of these elements will be involved:

- Voluntary contact
- Stop
- Frisk
- Plain feel
- Consent search
- Search
- Issue of citation
- Custodial arrest
- Search incident to arrest

These events must happen in a certain order, and each action must be constitutionally permissible (legal).

For example:

| *Stop* ⟶ *Frisk* ⟶ *Arrest* ⟶ *Search incident to arrest* |

or:

| *Voluntary Contact* ⟶ *Consent Frisk* ⟶ *Arrest* |

74

5 Legal Requirements

Understand the Sequence of an Arrest

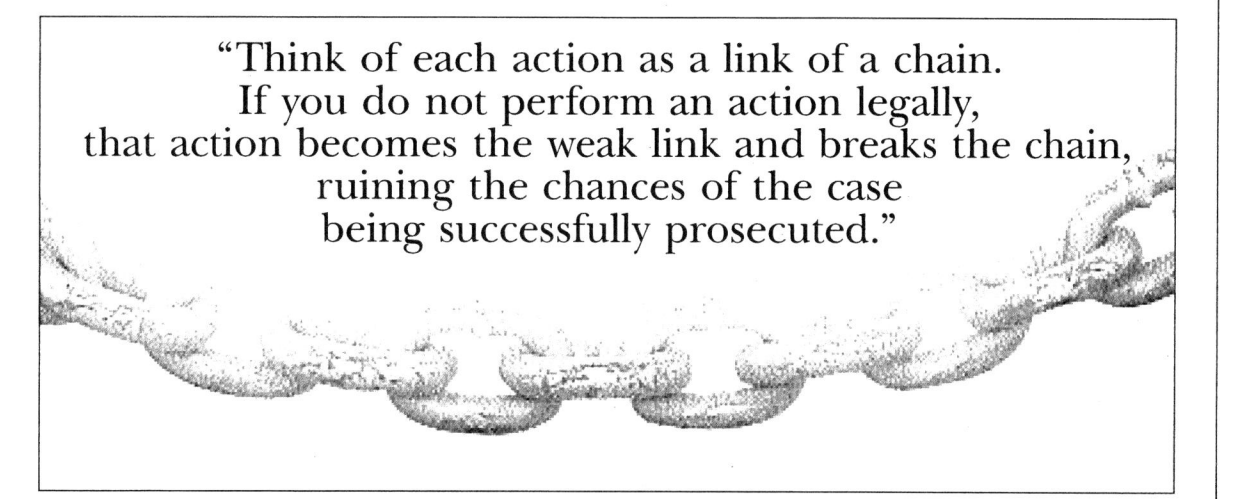

This was stated at the beginning of the chapter, but bears repeating:

> "Think of each action as a link of a chain. If you do not perform an action legally, that action becomes the weak link and breaks the chain, ruining the chances of the case being successfully prosecuted."

For example, if you illegally stop someone and he then tells you he has cocaine in his pocket as you are beginning to frisk him, the initial illegal seizure will result in the suppression of the evidence of cocaine even though he "volunteered" the information regarding it. The end result is wasted effort.

| **Illegal Stop** | The case stops here! | Frisk ⟶ Arrest |

LERC Report Writing

Understand the Sequence of an Arrest

What's wrong with this report?

Officer Baker and I were walking down 3rd Street at the intersection of Bull Avenue when we spotted a group of teenage males standing in a circle. This is an area where I have made numerous arrests and confiscated many drugs. As we approached this group, they all disbanded, except a black male pocketing some money. We ordered him to stop and did a frisk for officer safety. We recovered two small marijuana cigarettes from a plastic bag in his sock. The defendant was arrested. We searched him incident to that arrest and found two small rocks of cocaine in his pocket.

answers on next page

5 Legal Requirements

What's wrong with this report:

1. *The officers ordered the suspect to stop.*
There is no legal basis for the stop. Ordering a person to stop is a seizure even if the person was already stopped (standing still). At this point there is no legal basis for detaining.

In order to stop someone, there must be reasonable articulable suspicion that the suspect was engaged in or about to engage in criminal activity. What was the suspect doing that was illegal? Where are the facts in the police report to support such a conclusion?

Standing on the street putting money into your pocket is not a crime in any jurisdiction. The officer failed to articulate sufficient reasons to justify this stop. The suspect could argue that he felt he had to stop and wasn't free to leave—a violation of his 4th amendment rights.

What if the officers had asked the subject if they could talk to him? Officers do not need any reason to engage citizens in "voluntary contacts" as long as the citizen reasonably believes he is free to leave. The officers could then gather facts that would justify further legal actions.

2. *...frisk for officer safety*
Nothing in the report gives us reason to believe the defendant was armed and dangerous. The report states "I did a frisk for officer safety." This boiler plate language is insufficient to justify the frisk. Frisking as a routine practice of protecting yourself cannot be justified under the 4th amendment. It does not meet the legal requirement that you articulate specific reasons to be concerned for your safety. You must be able to give objective reasons you believed the suspect might be armed or presently dangerous.

If the stop is no good, then the evidence obtained in the frisk will be suppressed as the "fruits of the poisonous tree."

3. *We recovered two marijuana cigarettes...*
There is no explanation for how the officer lawfully found the marijuana when he was conducting a frisk for weapons. A frisk is conducted for weapons only. An officer may only seize other contraband during a frisk for weapons if it is immediately apparent to the officer that the item was contraband (known as plain feel exception to the search warrant requirement).

Understand the Sequence of an Arrest

Understand the Sequence of an Arrest

Let's look at the previous example. If the incident happened exactly as described, the stop was unjustified. Since the stop was illegal, any actions that follow become irrelevant.

However, if there is information that was left out, the problem becomes one of faulty report writing instead of poor police work.

Now read about the same arrest from Officer Baker's report.

Officer Baker's Report

At roll call at the beginning of our shift, Officer Mitchell and I were informed of citizen complaints of illegal gambling and drug activity in a lot beside M&M Grocery on 3rd Street. This is an area where I have made numerous arrests and confiscated many drugs.

At about 5:30 p.m., Officer Mitchell and I were walking down 3rd Street at the intersection of Bull Avenue when we spotted a group of teenage males standing in a circle in the lot by the grocery. As we approached, they all quickly walked away, except for a man hurriedly stuffing cash into his pants pocket. He had a large number of bills in his left hand and was sticking money into his pocket with his right hand so quickly that some was falling to the ground. I also saw a pair of dice fall from his pocket.

I recognized him as Samuel Fears, a man I had arrested before for street gambling and drug possession. I also knew he had been arrested with a concealed gun two months ago. Officer Mitchell ordered him to stop and conducted a frisk. No weapons were found. I asked Fears what he had been doing and he said, "Nothing." I asked him where he got the money and he said he picked it up off the ground.

I asked him if I could search him more closely and he said, "Sure, ain't illegal to have money." During the search I felt a plastic bag in his right sock. I removed the bag from the sock and found it contained heroin.

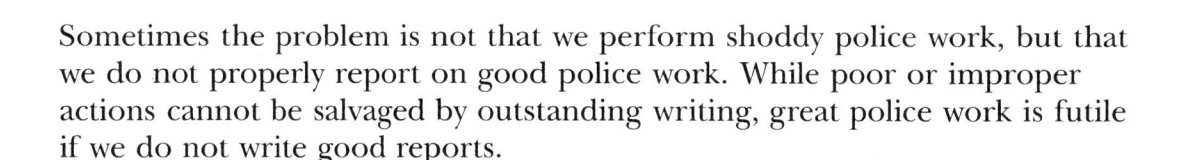

Sometimes the problem is not that we perform shoddy police work, but that we do not properly report on good police work. While poor or improper actions cannot be salvaged by outstanding writing, great police work is futile if we do not write good reports.

5 Legal Requirements

▶ C. Use a "Legal Checklist" When Writing Your Report.

Every action you take must be supported by facts that establish the legal justification for your actions (e.g., stop, frisk, search, issue a citation, or arrest). Always strive to prepare such an outstanding report that the defense attorney who reads it prefers to cop a plea rather than take the case to trial.

Use a "checklist" of legal requirements when writing your reports. Include:

- venue, the place where the crime occurred

- legal basis for the encounter or stop established (voluntary contact or reasonable, articulable suspicion)

- legal basis for frisks or searches (Did you fully articulate the legal basis for discovery of drugs during a pat frisk for weapons?)

- probable cause for arrest (all the elements of the crime listed)

- legal basis for search

- statements obtained from all witnesses

- full Miranda warning and waiver (if applicable)

- statements obtained from suspect

- why arrest was necessary instead of issuing a citation (when you find contraband in a search related to the arrest)

- list of evidence and its disposition (inventory)

- identification of all officers who had knowledge of the case

Look at the totality of the circumstances. List all the factors you relied upon to justify your actions. Every fact you considered must be in your police report. If it's not in your report, it will carry no weight with a prosecutor or judge.

Use a "Legal Checklist" When Writing Your Report

The Broken Link

Here is another actual police report. Use the legal checklist and find the bad link in the legal chain:

On 8-14-15 I was working Squad 404 with Officer Mesker. At 0022 hours we were dispatched to Gas 'n Go at 925 Hart Street in the report of an employee theft. The remarks of the call stated the theft occurred on 08-01-15.

Upon arrival, officers met with the manager (Mike Nelson) in the store. He told officers he had an employee, Kyle Thompson, who stole a minimum of $40.00 in merchandise to include 2 packs of an unknown brand of beer and a carton of Newport cigarettes. The manager informed us the theft of the beer was on video tape. He also stated that the suspect employee admitted to stealing the cigarettes after being confronted with the video tape capturing the theft of the beer. The suspect employee was back in the storage room.

Officers went to the back storage room with Nelson. Officers observed Thompson standing in the storage room. I approached Thompson and asked if he had any identification. He provided me with a Military Active Duty identification card. It showed he exited the military in April 2014.

Knowing that Thompson was a Gas 'n Go employee, part of his job would be to stock shelves and dispose of garbage. I possibly believed that he could be carrying some type of cutting instrument that could be used as a weapon. I quickly frisked his outer clothing. When I frisked the area over his right front pants pocket I noticed 2 hard metal objects that I believed to be possible weapons. I thought these hard objects could possibly be folding pocket knives. I reached into his pants pocket and retrieved the 2 objects which turned out to be 2 stainless steel cigarette lighters. These lighters were much heavier than a regular plastic cigarette lighter.

As I was removing the lighters from his pocket the inner part of my wrist hit a bulge in his left coin pocket which is inside of the larger pants pocket. I looked at the coin pocket and observed a US currency bill balled up. From my past experiences and training I have found that people are known to use and carry narcotics in paper money in a fashion similar to this. I looked at the bill and asked Thompson what he had inside it. He replied, "Powder." I then asked him, "Is it meth?" He then replied by nodding his head up and down. I then removed the bill and observed 2 rocks of suspected crack cocaine. (Report continues with booking and evidence information)

5 Legal Requirements

Pretty well written? Yes.

Pretty thorough? Complete facts and details? On the surface, yes.

The broken link:
The County Attorney's Office explains why the case was denied:

According to the police report, Officer Mesker frisked Thompson because he had a job of stocking shelves and disposing of garbage. Therefore Thompson could be carrying some type of cutting instrument that could be used as a weapon. These are insufficient facts to believe Thompson is armed. There are no facts that Thompson ever used or carried a cutting instrument. Therefore, the frisk could not be justified and the drugs would be suppressed. As an alternative, a search incident to arrest might have been made with sufficient evidence. First, the report would need to outline probable cause for a theft. The police report does not include date and time of the theft. Second, the report would need to state why an arrest would be necessary for a misdemeanor.

The link? When the search was deemed illegal, the case stopped there.

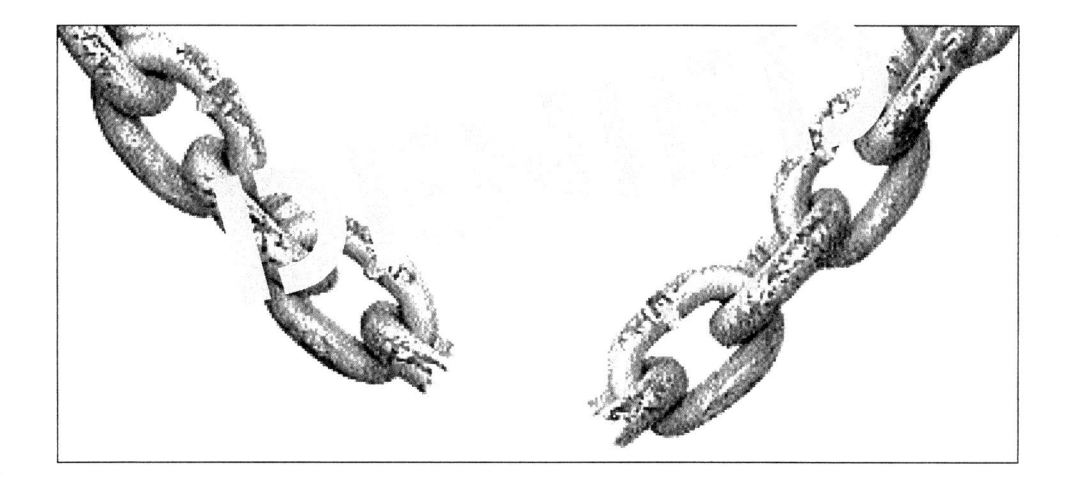

Use a "Legal Checklist" When Writing Your Report

81

Use a "Legal Checklist" When Writing Your Report

Look at your report from the point of view of a defense attorney.
Where is the weak link to attack? Cases are often thrown out because the initial stop was illegal. The stop was either not reasonable, or not articulated. Some cases are thrown out for illegal frisks—You pulled him over for speeding, frisked him and found a gun—wait a minute, what's your reason for frisking a speeder??? Look at the link of the chain. If there was no probable cause for a prostitution arrest, there is no way you'll be able to prosecute for possession of drugs found in a search incident to the arrest.

Use your report to improve your police work.
Find out which cases were successfully prosecuted and which were not. In the cases which fail, could you have improved your police work, or did your report let you down?

It's often a combination of factors that makes the difference to the prosecutor or the judge in deciding whether you had a legal basis for your police actions. Don't get lazy when it's time to justify your actions in your reports. Eventually you will be stuck with your report when you have to justify your actions in court testimony.

It's not just what you did or what happened that matters—it's what you put in your report that counts. Everything you did is important—don't just assume you put enough facts in your report.

You took the time to stop the suspect, frisk or search him, arrest him and find contraband on him. Take the few extra minutes it takes when writing your report to make successful prosecution possible.

5 Legal Requirements

CHECK YOUR OWN WRITING

Directions: Look over the incident report you wrote at the beginning of the training ("The Call," pages 8-9).

What legal issues were addressed in the report?

_____
_____
_____
_____
_____
_____
_____

Check Your Own Writing

Notes:

Chapter 6
Writing the DUI/DWI Report

> **OBJECTIVES**
> - Establish the legal basis for your actions.
> - Clearly describe the elements of the offense of DUI/DWI.
> - Understand the DUI/DWI report format.
> - Write the DUI/DWI report.

Whether it's called DUI or DWI in your state, drunk driving is a serious threat to public safety. The successful prosecution of the case depends upon your ability to organize and present your observations in writing. Many state statutes contain the following language:

It is unlawful for any person to operate or be in actual physical control of any vehicle upon roadways, "lands," or waterways of this state while under the influence of alcohol or any drug.

Establish the legal basis for your actions.
Your observations during a DWI investigation are extremely important. You must be able to establish the level of impairment at the time the violation occurred. Subsequent evidence of impairment, such as the evidential chemical tests, will be admissible only when a proper arrest has been made.

Clearly describe the elements of the offense of DUI/DWI.
There are three phases of DUI/DWI detection.
- Observation of the vehicle in motion
- Personal contact with the driver
- Pre-arrest screening

Understand the DUI/DWI report format.
Use suggested headings to create the DUI/DWI Report.

Write the DUI/DWI report.
Write your own DUI/DWI Report and compare to ours.

Establish the Legal Basis for Your Actions

A. Establish the Legal Basis for Your Actions

The collection of evidence during a DWI investigation is like a series of stepping stones. Unless you have a legal basis to move to the next stone, any evidence you find will be inadmissible. For example, without sufficient grounds for a stop, the field sobriety tests, suspect's admissions, and breath test will all be inadmissible, effectively sinking your case.

You must document:

- Sufficient grounds for stopping or contacting the accused.

- The accused was the operator or in actual physical control of the vehicle.

- Sufficient cause to believe that the accused was impaired.

- That proper regard was given to suspect's rights.

- That additional observation and interview of the suspect provided evidence relevant to the alleged offense.

- Reasonable grounds for arrest.

- That chemical test was properly requested and administered.

6 Writing the DUI/DWI Report

The prosecutor's case will largely be based upon the officer's investigation as reflected in the arrest report. If all of the above elements are not established in the report, your case may be lost before you ever get to court. The prosecutor can amend, reduce, or even dismiss the case on the basis of the arrest report alone.

It is not enough to observe and recognize symptoms of impaired driving. You must paint a picture of the violator through your report to present a clear image of the evidence.

Your investigation of a suspected drunk driver should be conducted as if no breath or blood test will be given. Evidence collection should occur throughout the entire encounter with the driver.

Establish the Legal Basis for Your Actions

▶ B. Clearly Describe the Elements of the DUI/DWI Offense

There are three phases of DUI/DWI detection.

- Observation of the vehicle in motion
- Personal contact with the driver
- Pre-arrest screening

You must describe your observations clearly and in a manner that convinces a judge or jury to draw the same conclusion you did—that the driver was under the influence.

87

LERC *Report Writing*

Clearly Describe the Elements of the DUI/DWI Offense

Directions: Watch the video "The DUI/DWI Stop," taking notes on the evidence you see of driver impairment.

Note: The sobriety tests may be performed somewhat differently in your state.

6 Writing the DUI/DWI Report

Now read Officer Murray's report:

On 11-15-15

at 21:15 I, Officer Murray, was northbound on Hampshire Avenue at Bush Lake Rd. I saw a maroon Saturn MN DSS122 in front of me. The car was driving erratically all over the road. I turned on my lights to stop the car and it took awhile for the driver to see me and stop.

I approached the driver and got his license. His name was Daniel O'Neal (DOB 8-14-83). I could smell a strong odor of alcoholic beverage on his breath. He appeared to be drunk. I asked him to get out of his car for some field sobriety tests.

I administered several field sobriety tests. (See attached field notes form.) O'Neal performed the tests in a way that caused me to conclude he was intoxicated. I arrested him for DWI.

Later at the police station, he refused the breath test offered by Sgt. Nix.

Clearly Describe the Elements of the DUI/DWI Offense

LERC Report Writing

Clearly Describe the Elements of the DUI/DWI Offense

PHASE 1. Observation of the Vehicle in Motion

What direction was O'Neal's car traveling? _doesn't say_
Is this evident in the Officer Murray's report? _yes_

The officer describes the car as "driving erratically." Can you provide a clearer, more specific description of the vehicle's movements before the stop?

_____
_____
_____
_____
_____
_____
_____

6 Writing the DUI/DWI Report

A better description might read something like this:

The left tires of the car were over the yellow double lane stripes. He weaved to the right, across the left lane and into the right lane for about 20 feet. Next, he weaved back to the left for about 30 feet. His tires were over the double lines by 2 feet for about 15 feet. He weaved back to the right lane for about 40 feet, then back to the left for about 20 feet and over the double lines again by 2 feet for about 15 feet. The car weaved back to the right lane for about 30 feet, then back again to the left for another 20 feet and over the double yellow lines again. This time he went so far over the yellow lines that his right tires touched them.

I turned on my emergency lights and he began pull to the right. After about one block he pulled along the curb, braked, rolled forward slowly, and stopped.

This description may sound excessive, but such detail convinces a prosecutor—and the defense attorney—that you have a good case. It certainly provides a better description than "driving erratically."

Clearly Describe the Elements of the DUI/DWI Offense

91

LERC *Report Writing*

Clearly Describe the Elements of the DUI/DWI Offense

Do you know the difference between *weaving, drifting,* and *swerving?* These are all words that describe common driving behaviors exhibited by drunk drivers. Your report must clearly describe the driver's behavior.

WEAVING
The vehicle alternately moves toward one side of the lane and then the other. The pattern of lateral movement can be fairly regular as one steering correction is closely followed by another.

DRIFTING
The vehicle moves in a generally straight line, but at a slight angle to the lane. The driver might correct course as the vehicle approaches a lane line or other boundary, or fail to correct until after the boundary has been crossed.

SWERVING
The vehicle makes an abrupt turn away from a generally straight course when the driver realizes that the car has drifted out of proper lane position, or to avoid a previously undetected hazard.

Is the report's use of "weaving" to describe the vehicle movement correct?   YES ✗
                                                                                NO ____

PHASE 2. Personal Contact with the Driver

Officer Murray's report says the driver "appeared to be drunk." Is this description specific enough? What information from the video could you add to "paint a picture" of the driver's physical condition for those who will read the report?

_____
_____
_____
_____
_____
_____
_____

6 Writing the DUI/DWI Report

Clearly Describe the Elements of the DUI/DWI Offense

Check to see if you included:

- Driver would not make eye contact with officer.
- Getting out of car he put his hand on the car for balance once.
- Driver swayed from side to side as he stood facing the officer.

Other facts not visible on video include:

- Driver's eyes were bloodshot.
- He smelled of alcohol.

PHASE 3. Pre-Arrest Screening

Officer Murray wrote that he administered field sobriety tests, but did not provide any details.

I administered several field sobriety tests. O'Neal performed the tests in a way that caused me to conclude he was intoxicated. I arrested him for DWI.

Later at the police station, he refused the breath test offered by Sgt. Nix.

Clearly Describe the Elements of the DUI/DWI Offense

Some officers feel that including an attached Field Sobriety Test form is adequate. It is not. Think of your trips to the doctor. The doctor makes notes on a standard form which includes weight, blood pressure, heart rate, etc. If you were to read a medical report, however, you would find that there is much more information included than what is on these "check-off" forms. The doctor includes his or her observations of your behavior, demeanor, and physical symptoms in order to prepare a complete report of your condition. This is what you must strive for in your DUI/DWI report.

Again, your investigation of a suspected drunk driver should be conducted as if no breath or blood test will be given.

The prosecutor must be able to establish that the defendant was driving or could put a vehicle in motion while under the influence of alcohol or drugs.

In most jurisdictions the state must prove that the driver was in physical control of the vehicle. You might establish "driving" or "physical control" through your observations. Be sure to note:

- the location of the vehicle
- location of defendant inside of vehicle
- whether the vehicle was recently operated
- location of keys
- location of other occupants
- witness statements

6 Writing the DUI/DWI Report

If an accident has occurred and the passengers are all out of the vehicle, you may have to rely on witnesses, physical evidence, or the suspect's statements to place the driver behind the wheel.

Don't get in such a hurry to "cuff'em and stuff'em" that you fail to obtain witnesses' names, names of the occupants of the suspect's vehicle, and any other evidence that might be helpful to the prosecutor.

In addition to showing who was operating a vehicle, you must prove "intoxication" or "under the influence." The best way is to collect and document evidence as if no chemical test will occur. Many officers take the easy way out and gloss over sobriety tests and other evidence because a high blood alcohol reading was obtained on a chemical test. Chemical tests are sometimes ruled inadmissible in court, and many drivers will refuse to take such tests. While a refusal can be used against the driver, there is no automatic assumption that the driver was intoxicated. You must still prove it through observations that are documented in your report.

Clearly Describe the Elements of the DUI/DWI Offense

Types of DUI/DWI Evidence presented in court:

- Documentation (e.g., the citation, the alcohol influence report, the drug evaluation report, evidential chemical test results, etc.).

- Testimony (the officer's verbal description of what was seen, heard, smelled, etc.).

- Physical (or real) evidence: something tangible, visible, audible (e.g., a blood sample or a partially empty can of beer).

- Well established facts (e.g. judicial notice of accuracy of the breath test device when proper procedures are followed).

- Demonstrative evidence: demonstrations performed in courtroom (e.g., field sobriety tests).

Think about how your testimony may be attacked. Was the defendant wearing high-heels, floppy sandals, or other footwear which might have hindered performance on the sobriety tests? Did the defendant have a physical disability or illness that might have affected performance? Find out the answers to these questions before administering the tests, and include the answers in your report.

C. Understand the DUI/DWI Report Format

Much of the evidence you collect during a DWI investigation is recorded on special forms, such as a field sobriety report. However, the narrative is still important. No standardized form can capture all the information regarding a drunk driver.

The following are suggested headings that can help you check off necessary information for your DWI report.

HEADINGS

Preliminary Information

Initial Observations

Vehicle Stop

Driver Contact

Field Sobriety Tests

Arrest

Disposition of Vehicle and Contents

Implied Consent

Final Disposition

Preliminary Information
Date, time and place of incident

Initial Observations
What brought the vehicle to your attention?

> Key Points:
> - What driving behaviors are seen?
> - Do you have probable cause to stop the vehicle?
> - Are there witnesses to the vehicle's operation?

Vehicle Stop
How does the driver react to your signal to stop?

> Key Points:
> - How does the driver handle the vehicle while stopping?
> - Additional observations:
>   Weather conditions
>   Road conditions
> - Names of passengers and location in vehicle
> - Statements:
>   Driver
>   Passenger(s)
>   Witness(es)

6 Writing the DUI/DWI Report

Driver Contact
General driver appearance

- Bloodshot eyes
- Slurred speech when questioned
- Smell of alcoholic beverages
- Soiled clothing
- Coordination upon exit

Evidence observed

- Alcohol beverage containers
- Drugs or drug paraphernalia

Field Sobriety Tests
Specifics on each test

- Walk and Turn
- One Leg Stand
- Horizontal Gaze Nystagmus
- Other tests

Do I have probable cause for arrest?

Is the impairment from drugs, alcohol, illness or a combination?
Does driver have any handicaps which may affect test?
Is driver wearing footwear which may affect test?

Arrest

Key Points:
- Implied Consent
- Time of arrest and time of departure for evidential testing
- Chemical Test
- Defendant's Statement

Disposition of Vehicle and Occupants

Key Points:
- Vehicle disposition—towed, locked, released
- Temporary driver's license
- Citations/Charge Sheet
- Released/Held
- Disposition of passengers

Implied Consent

Key Points:
- Rights form/implied consent warning—witnesses?
- Type of test offered and given. Who administered test?
- Defendant's response, (took test, refused test)
- Chain of custody if bodily fluid was sampled
- Additional test requested or given?

Final Disposition

Key Points:
- Defendant incarcerated?
- Nature and disposition of physical evidence

Understand the DUI/DWI Report Format

D. Write the DUI/DWI Report

Write the DUI/DWI Report

The DUI/DWI Report

6 Writing the DUI/DWI Report

Write the DUI/DWI Report

Write the DUI/DWI Report

6 Writing the DUI/DWI Report

Preliminary Paragraph
On 11-15-15 at 2115 hours, I was on routine patrol, traveling north on Hampshire Ave. I was driving a marked squad car (#824).

Initial Observations
I saw a maroon Saturn MN DSS122 also traveling north on Hampshire Ave, at Bush Lake Rd. It was in front of me in the left lane. The left tires of the car were over the yellow double lane stripes. He weaved to the right, across the left lane and into the right lane for about 20 feet. Next, he weaved back to the left for about 30 feet. His tires were over the double lines by 2 feet for about 15 feet. He weaved back to the right lane for about 40 feet, then back to the left for about 20 feet and over the double lines again by 2 feet for about 15 feet. The car weaved back to the right lane for about 30 feet, then back again to the left for another 20 feet and over the double yellow lines again. This time he went so far over the yellow lines that his right tires touched them.

Vehicle Stop
I turned on my emergency lights and he began pull to the right. After about one block he pulled along the curb, braked, rolled forward slowly, and stopped.

The weather was clear. It was dark out. The road conditions were normal.

I approached the vehicle. He did not look at me so I tapped on the window. He rolled the window down, but would still not make eye contact.

Driver Contact
I asked the driver, Daniel O'Neal (DOB 8-14-83), for his license. He asked, "What's this for?" I smelled alcohol coming from his breath as he spoke and noticed his eyes were bloodshot. He took his wallet out and handed me his license. I asked him if he had anything to drink and he said, "I had a drink or two of beer."

I asked him if he would perform field sobriety tests and he agreed. As he exited his car he was unstable and swayed, touching the car once to regain his balance as he walked toward my squad car. I asked him to stand in front of my squad car facing his car so that my emergency lights would not affect his ability to perform the test. He swayed and moved his feet to keep balance while I was giving him instructions.

Field Sobriety Tests
I told him that he would be performing the standardized field sobriety field tests. I asked if there was any reason that he could not perform the test, and if he had any problems or handicaps. He replied "No" to both questions. He was wearing brown work boots.

Compare Your Report

The first test was the walk and turn: 9 out and 9 back. I explained the test and he said he understood the directions.
> He was unable to keep his balance during instruction.
> His arms were up 45 degrees.
> He was unable to hold his feet in the proper position.
> As he walked forward he did not touch his heel to toe.
> The gap was approximately 3-6 inches on all his steps.
> He was off line on his 3,4,5, and 7 steps.
> He used his arms for balance the entire walk out.
> He took an incorrect number of steps; he performed 10.
> He failed to pivot on return.

On the return he:
> Failed to touch heel to toe, 3-6 inch gaps.
> Was off line on 2,3,4-7; stopped at nine.
> Swayed as he walked, using arms for balance, 45 degrees.

The next test was the one leg stand. I explained the test and he said he understood the directions.
> He raised his leg up then put foot down at 4,6,10,11,15.
> He was unable to complete the 2nd try, hopping and using his arms for balance at 45 degrees.
> He kept touching the squad car for balance.
> He was unable to continue a third try.

Horizontal gaze nystagmus was administered.
> All six clues were detected.

A preliminary breath test was not available at the scene of the stop.

Arrest:
I placed O'Neal under arrest, put him in my squad, and took him to the station for booking.

Disposition of Vehicle and Occupants:
O'Neal's car was towed to the city impound lot.

Implied Consent
Later, at the police station, he refused the breath test offered by Sgt. Nix.

Final Disposition
O'Neal was held at the city jail, until released into custody of his brother.

Note:
The previous report follows the format on pages 96-97. We know that departments differ in the way they process DUI's or, for that matter, Incident/Offense Reports. For example, some departments would put an Intoxilyzer test under the Implied Consent heading. Others might put it under the Disposition heading.

It is important to develop a format which works for your department. Organizing reports by using headings will make your reports easy to write, easy to read, and very useful to investigators and city and county attorneys.

6 Writing the DUI/DWI Report

Conclusion

Why did we devote an entire chapter to DUI/DWI?

You save lives when you remove drunk drivers from the road.

It's as simple as that. Your observations of the driver's behavior are crucial to the prosecution of the case.

Combine the report writing skills you've learned here with your already fine police work, and you will increase your convictions of drunk drivers.

Notes:

CHAPTER 7
Writing the Domestic Violence Report

OBJECTIVES

- Find out who reads a police report.
- Understand how a domestic violence report differs from other reports.
- Clearly describe evidence establishing domestic violence.
- Understand the domestic violence report format.

Please note: Statutes regarding domestic violence vary from state to state. Some information supplied here may not apply in your state. The concepts, however, remain the same. Report headings are meant to be a guide (not a rigid template) to creating your own report forms.

Find out who reads a police report.
The police report is arguably the most important document in a domestic violence case. Many different people rely on it to make decisions. This section will expand your understanding of who reads your reports. It will help you go beyond simply documenting an incident for the prosecutor. You'll see how you are part of a coordinated community response.

Understand how a domestic violence report differs from other reports.
Most victims of crimes want to see the perpetrators of those crimes convicted. This is often not the case for victims of domestic violence. Why is that? They are generally emotionally and financially attached to their abusers, and they are well aware that any legal action taken may result in more hostility and violence towards themselves or their children.

Clearly describe evidence establishing domestic violence.
It takes all of your police skills to determine who should be arrested in a domestic violence case. The victim may later refuse to testify, or change the story. Determining the predominant aggressor, assessing self-defense, and using exceptions to the hearsay rule will help build a solid case.

Understand the Domestic Violence report format.
Use suggested headings as a guide to your report.

LERC Report Writing

Find Out Who Reads a Police Report

> **A. Find Out Who Reads a Police Report**

Police Report: Law Enforcement Agency, Follow-up Investigators, Attorneys, Judge, Responding Officer, Victims, Civil Court, Probation Officer, Advocates, News Media

The Law Enforcement Agency
- To determine the completeness of the report, probable cause for arrest, and if further investigation is needed.

Follow-up Investigators
- To see what details need to be further explored and to decide whether to alert the prosecutor to pursue higher charges.

Attorneys
- The prosecutor, to determine the charges and whether or not to pursue the case. The defense attorney, to find the weak link and destroy the case.

Judges
- To determine the conditions of bail and/or release, issue protective orders, or restrict access to children.

Responding Officers
- You may use it in court when you testify. You will use it to reinforce what happened and the actions you took. If the victim recants, the case may rely totally on your testimony.

The Victim
- For information on disposition of suspect, and to check accuracy of report.

Civil Court
- To determine if a protection order should be granted, and what arrangements should be made for visitation.

The Probation Officer
- To prepare the pre-sentence investigation for the court to determine appropriate consequences.

Advocates
- Advocacy staff and counselors who work with victims and offenders, along with the child protection agency, to determine the needs of any children involved.

News Media
- To get the story straight.

7 Writing the Domestic Violence Report

When you write a domestic violence report, it doesn't simply end up on a supervisor's desk. You are part of a coordinated community response. This does not mean that your report has to be a virtual thesis rather than a short two pages. But keep in mind the skills you have practiced in the previous chapters. Will your report give the follow-up investigator a clear idea of what happened? Can the prosecuting attorney quickly locate the facts? Will the child protection investigators understand your language? Make it possible for other members of the community to do their jobs efficiently.

How a Domestic Violence Report Differs

▶ B. Understand How a Domestic Violence Report Differs from Other Reports

How is it that a domestic violence report differs from the reports we have done so far? Don't we write the same kind of complete report we would for any other crime? Well, yes, but domestic violence reports *are* different from other reports:

You must prepare your report as if it is a murder case and the victim is not available to testify.
Unfortunately, it is very possible that the victim will not testify in court, or that the story will have changed significantly since the arrest. A vast majority of the information used for prosecution will come from your first contact with the victim. Follow-up investigation is often fruitless. You usually can't go back and get more information at a later date. Your job is to convince the court that the first story was <u>the</u> story.

It is important to document the emotional state and demeanor of both suspect and victim.
In the DUI/DWI chapter we emphasized the importance of documenting the movement of the vehicle as well as the behavior of the suspect. The behavior and demeanor of both suspect and victim are important to the domestic violence case. Officers sometimes fail to include their observations in reports even though they were later able to list behaviors that made them believe abuse was going on:

107

How a Domestic Violence Report Differs

"He wouldn't let her out of his sight when we were there."
"He was yelling at her–telling her what to say when she was talking to me..."
"She was obviously scared of him–she kept glancing over to see if he could hear her."

These are observations that prosecutors and others need in order to get a picture of what the officer sensed at the scene. Include them in your report.

Evidence is often subtle and non-physical.
Victims are often reluctant to discuss their injuries. Strangulation victims often have no immediate visible signs of physical assault. Threats are often non-verbal.

"When I said I would call the police he made a motion with his finger across his neck–like slitting a throat."

Good investigators will keep pursuing an interview to gain as much information as possible.

Documenting the time of statements is critical.
Exceptions to the hearsay rule are important in domestic violence prosecution. Timing is everything. Hang on, we'll explore this in the next section.

Accurate contact information is vital.
Prosecutors, victim advocates, probation officers and others often have trouble contacting the victim. Include contact information for at least two people who can always get in touch for the victim.

Note: This should <u>not</u> be part of the report narrative, since the suspect will also have access to the information. This information can often be included in confidential records such as a Request for Commitment jail form or a similar form.

The report is very important even if no arrest is made.
Domestic abuse is a patterned offense where violence often escalates. The first or second well-written domestic report may not stop the violence in a particular family but the third or fourth often will. Many times the police report is the only evidence documenting the history of abuse. Do not underestimate the importance of your report writing. The bottom line is, you may ultimately save lives.

7 Writing the Domestic Violence Report

Documenting future risk is important.

Do you think he or she will seriously injure or kill you or your children? How frequently does he or she intimidate, threaten, or assault you? Describe the most frightening event/worst incidence of violence involving him/her.

These risk questions help determine the victim's level of danger. Responses should be in your report.

Domestic abuse victims are vulnerable to eventual serious assault and/or murder. Lives are at stake whenever you take a domestic violence call.

> **C. Clearly Describe Evidence Establishing Domestic Violence.**

As a law enforcement officer, you are the eyes and ears of the entire legal system. You observe things that no one else can. No one else sees the context in which the violence occurs. No one else senses the fear present the night of an assault. No one else talks to the victim immediately after an incident, when she may be most willing to talk about what really happened. No one else sees the children at the scene, their relationship to the violence, and the danger they face. No one else encounters the offender before he or she is prepared for a court hearing by the defense. Your description of the initial encounter is absolutely vital to the case.

An officer makes three primary determinations on a domestic abuse related call:

- was there probable cause?
- did any party act in self-defense?
- if there is probable cause to arrest both parties, who is the predominant aggressor?

While it is beyond the scope of this course to train you in the methods of investigating domestic violence, it is important that you realize the importance of pursuing evasive interviewees until these questions are answered. An officer who throws up his hands and says, "I'll arrest them both and let the courts sort it out" has done nothing.

In the second part of this section we'll look at how to document statements, and how exceptions to the hearsay rule can help you.

Describe Evidence Establishing Domestic Violence

Describe Evidence Establishing Domestic Violence

Establishing Probable Cause

State statutes defining domestic abuse may vary somewhat, but often include:

- physical harm, bodily injury or assault
- the infliction of fear or imminent physical harm, bodily injury or assault
- terroristic threats
- criminal sexual conduct committed against a family or household member by a family or household member

The officer must consider the **totality of the circumstances** when making a probable cause determination. The totality of circumstances includes:

- information received from 911
- officer observations which corroborate or dispute accounts
- physical evidence at the scene
- either party's history of abusive behavior
- the officer's interpretation of the information–educated decisions based on training and experience.

Considering some factors and ignoring others can lead to an inappropriate arrest and a thrown out case. If you choose not to arrest, your reasons should be clearly stated in your report.

Documenting Evidence of Self-Defense

In domestic violence cases it is common for both parties to claim to be the victim. There are four important points regarding self-defense:

1. The person using force had a reasonable belief that he or she was at risk of bodily harm.
Ask questions like, "What were you thinking when you picked up the frying pan?" If the person responds, "I wasn't going to let him come near me," ask "Why? What did you think would happen?" (Force cannot be used to prevent emotional abuse.) Quote the person when possible.

2. The risk of harm is actual or imminent.
The risk cannot be for some undetermined time in the future, as in, "Someday I'm going to whip your ass."

3. The use of force was reasonably necessary to prevent the infliction of bodily harm.
The standard here is about the level of force, not its effectiveness.

4. The use of force is based on the beliefs that person has about the above issues at the time of the incident, not on the intent of the person making the threat.

7 Writing the Domestic Violence Report

In almost all cases of domestic abuse, one party is using violence as a pattern of coercion and intimidation, and the other is reacting to that violence. In almost all cases one person is far less able to stop the violence against her/him.

Offensive vs. Defensive Wounds
Investigating officers need to carefully distinguish offensive and defensive wounds such as bite marks and scratches. Physical injuries and the use or presence of weapons in a self-defense context are often misinterpreted.

Scratches and bites on the body most often appear on male perpetrators when they use their strength to physically subdue and dominate a female victim, and she struggles to get away. Ironically, a strangulation attack will often result in very little or no physical evidence on the victim, but the attacker frequently has scratches on his arms or face.

A female victim may have scratches on her neck or upper chest that appear to be self-inflicted, but actually occurred when the victim struggled to remove the attacker's stranglehold. Other injuries on women such as bruises on the back, the buttocks, or the backside of arms and legs are indicative of an aggressive attack, typically while the victim was in a defensive or fetal position. Injuries of this nature tend to show that the other party was more likely the predominant aggressor.

Be specific in your descriptions.
Sandra Delaney said she bit her husband while he pinned her against the door. Jack Delaney had a 2-inch red mark in the middle of his chest right below his neck.

Determining the Predominant Aggressor

> A *predominant aggressor* is defined as:
> *"the party to the incident who, by their actions in this incident and through known history and actions, has caused the most fear and intimidation against the other."*

Determining the predominant aggressor is often a difficult task. The predominant aggressor is the most dangerous aggressor, not necessarily the first aggressor. You cannot just say, "Well, A hit B first, so A is obviously the predominant aggressor." You must answer the question, "Who poses the greatest threat or likelihood of future harm?" Again, you must consider the totality of circumstances in making this determination. Good investigators will keep an interview going until the question is answered.

Describe Evidence Establishing Domestic Violence

LERC Report Writing

Describe Evidence Establishing Domestic Violence

More on Documentation
As you can imagine, documenting evidence which will stand up later in court is going to be hard. Here are some tools which will help you.

Formal Statements as Evidence
Some agencies use video or audio to record the victim's statement at the scene. This establishes an excellent record of the victim's account of the violence. Pictures can show any injuries to victims and damage to the premises by the perpetrator. Audio recordings can capture fear and emotional stress.

Written statements are also used. Obtain statements as soon as possible after the incident when victims and witnesses are more likely to be cooperative.

Offender statements are often neglected. A suspect in custody must be advised of the Miranda warning before you attempt to elicit a statement.

Information from neighbors, uninvolved household members, and other witnesses is often neglected. Be sure to talk to anyone who may have information on the incident. Canvass the neighborhood, if necessary.

Refer to all statements in your report. If the statements are in writing or have been recorded, summarize them in the report.

Using Hearsay Evidence

Many victims are reluctant witnesses. They do not want to testify about the abuse at a criminal trial for a variety of reasons. Victims may fear retribution. They may just want the whole matter to simply go away. Or they commonly will want to reconcile with their abuser.

Given the reluctance of a victim to cooperate with the justice system, a prosecutor may need to present evidence through other avenues.

A judge may allow exceptions to the hearsay rule under certain circumstances—and that makes the police report very important.

Hearsay evidence is simply testifying to what someone else has told you. The general rule is that hearsay is not admissible, but there are some exceptions that are valuable in domestic violence investigations. The following exceptions to the hearsay rule can help you when investigating a domestic violence case. Include these types of statements made by victims and suspects in your report.

Exceptions to the Hearsay Rule:

Excited Utterance: Federal Rule of Evidence 803 (2).
- The statement must relate to a startling event or condition.
- The statement must be made while the victim was under stress.
- The excitement must have been caused by the event.

The victim ran toward us, screaming, "He's going to kill me!

112

7 Writing the Domestic Violence Report

An excited utterance or spontaneous admission can be made by a suspect as well.

As I handcuffed him, he began crying and said, "I didn't mean to hurt her. I just wanted to stop her from leaving."

Document the exact time and nature of the excited statement and who witnessed it.

Present Sense Impression: Federal Rule of Evidence 803 (1).
- The statement must describe or explain an event.
- The statement must be made while the victim is experiencing the event or immediately afterward.

"My boyfriend just pulled a gun on me!"

The investigating officer should establish when the gun was pointed, as compared to the time the officer or dispatcher heard the statement from the victim.

Then Existing Mental, Emotional or Physical Condition: Federal Rule of Evidence 803 (3).
The rule covers three distinct categories of statements that are important to police when interviewing a witness:

- Statements of present bodily conditions
- Statements of present emotional state
- Statements of present state of mind

"My husband kicked me in the ribs. They hurt really bad— I think they are broken!"

Statements of present bodily conditions are admissible whether made to a physician, police officer, or other person. A victim's comment about her state of mind or emotional condition is important, such as a statement showing fear because of what the abuser has done. Such statements, if properly recorded, can be used to prove this element of the assault if the victim later recants.

> **D. Understand the Domestic Violence Report Format**

On the following pages are suggested headings that can help you check off necessary information for your Domestic Violence Report.

Describe Evidence Establishing Domestic Violence

Understand the Domestic Violence Report Format

HEADINGS
Preliminary Information
Officer's Observations
Victim Statements
Suspect Statements
Investigation of the Scene
Evidence Collected
Witness Statements
Children Present
Medical Treatment
Dangerous Suspect Assessment
Contact Information
Disposition

Preliminary Information
Noting time allows police to testify to what the victim said (exceptions to hearsay rule).
  Key Points:
  - Time of incident
  - Time of dispatch
  - Time of arrival
  - Time of first contact with victim

Officer's Observations
Helps jury picture what it was like at the time of the incident.
  Key Points:
  - Emotional state of victim
  - Emotional state of suspect
  - Description of visible injuries
  - Description of crime scene

Victim Statements
Helps prove the case if victim later recants or becomes uncooperative.
  Key Points:
  - "Excited utterances"
  - "Present sense impression"
  - "Then existing mental, emotional or physical condition"
    (exceptions to the hearsay rule)
  - Answers to risk questions

Suspect Statements
Detailed statements commit suspect to his version of the story, including who made first physical contact. It can be useful to dispute self-defense claims made later.

7 Writing the Domestic Violence Report

Investigation of the Scene
Makes incident more real for the jury.
Establishes violence.

Evidence Collected
(Photographs, bloody clothes etc.) Makes incident more real for the jury.

Witness Statements
Corroborates victim's statement; establishes elements of crime if victim refuses to testify.
  Key Points:
  - Statements from other household members
  - Statements from neighbors, onlookers
  - Emergency medical information

Children Present
Is used to decide needs for follow-up intervention on behalf of the children.
  Key Points:
  - Names/ages
  - Whereabouts
  - Were they directly involved in incident?
    (In some cases children may be used as witnesses.)

Medical Treatment
Medical evidence can be useful to prove case through corroborating victim's initial statements and establishing level of injuries.

Dangerous Suspect Assessment
Used to alert subsequent interveners to level of danger. Probation will use to determine release conditions and sentencing recommendations.
  Key Points:
  - Is violence escalating?
  - Is there access to guns?
  - Has suspect threatened to kill victim?

Contact Information
Used to locate victim/witness(es)/suspect and provide victim advocacy.
  Key Points:
  - Consider confidentiality issues.
    Include two people who can contact victim. Include as confidential supplement to report.

Disposition
  Key Points:
  - Arrest
  - Victim's rights
  - Victim advocacy information

Understand the Domestic Violence Report Format

No, we're not going to make you rewrite your whole report over again. But now that you know more about the domestic violence report, we want you to make sure you included these things:

What was the emotional state of both the victim and suspect?

What were the injuries?

What direct quotes should have been included?

Did you include disposition of the son?

What were the risk questions and their answers?

Where would you list contact information for Maryann?

7 Writing the Domestic Violence Report

CHECK YOUR OWN WRITING

Directions: Look over the incident report you wrote at the beginning of the training ("The Call," pages 8-9).

What additional information would you add to make this a complete domestic violence report?

Check Your Own Writing

LERC Report Writing

Write the Domestic Violence Report

Compare Your Report

Preliminary Information
Officers Smith and I, Officer Yournamehere, were dispatched at 1800 hours to 4932 Park Street. A neighbor heard a female yelling and screaming. We arrived at 1804 in Squad 24.

Officer's Observations
We were met at the door by Maryann McCarthy (DOB 4-17-78) and her husband Frank McCarthy (DOB 6-7-75). Maryann was upset, speaking rapidly with a raised voice, and near tears. When I interviewed her she seemed agitated and moved about in her chair. Frank was calm during his interview. Maryann had two 1-inch bruises on her right inner forearm, and a walnut-sized lump on the back of her head.

Victim Statement
Maryann said her son Timmy, 9, had come home an hour late, and this upset Frank. (She said she had told Timmy he could stay at a friend's for an extra hour.) She said she was afraid Frank would beat Timmy up, and pulled Frank away from Timmy. Maryann said Frank was "angry and out-of-control." She said she told Timmy to run away. She said Frank did not hit Timmy, but he has hit him in the past. Maryann said Frank grabbed her by the arms. She said, "He pushed me. He pushed me up against the wall. I hit my head on the wall." She said he then pushed her into a chair to try to calm her down. She said he slapped her across the right side of the face at least twice. She said he also knocked the lamp over, and pulled the phone out of the wall when she tried to call police.

Answers to risk questions:
Maryann said she was worried Frank may hurt himself. I asked if he had threatened to hurt himself in the past, and she said, "No."

I asked if Frank had any firearms in the house. She said he owns a handgun which he keeps in a box in the shed in the back yard.

I asked if he had ever threatened to kill her. She said he had not, but that he says he hates her and she is disgusting. She began crying when she said this. She said that after police come "he always says he won't do it again."

I asked if she noticed the abuse was getting worse. She said that Frank was most likely to use violence when he had been drinking. She said that bruises were "routine."

I asked her if she felt Frank was obsessed with her and had to always know what she was doing, where she going, etc. and she said, "All the time. Absolutely."

7 Writing the Domestic Violence Report

Suspect Statement
(Officer Smith interviewed Frank.) Frank said, "We just had a little argument. She's got a problem—we're taking care of it."

He said he had two beers to drink, but he was not intoxicated. Smith asked Frank if he had a "bit of a buzz," and he said, "Yeah, maybe, I don't know."

Officer Smith asked what started this. Frank said he thought Maryann was "messing around with somebody else." Smith asked him if he was really angry about this and Frank said, "I'm still angry about it."

Smith asked him if he may have put Maryann down in the chair too hard, and Frank said, "I didn't do anything wrong at all," and "I think you'd have done the same thing if your wife was doing this." Smith asked Frank, "Did you hit Maryann?" Frank said, "No." He said he did not push her to the ground.

Frank said Timmy was in the room but ran off because he was upset at his mother.

When asked about Maryann's behavior, Frank said, "She was coming at me crazy." He said she was swinging things around and took a swing at him. He said the only physical thing he did was hold her arms. He said, "I gotta stop her, I gotta control her, restrain her." Smith asked how Maryann got the bruises on her arm, and Frank said, "I don't know, she might have hurt herself. I was just trying to control her." Smith asked him how Maryann got the bump on her head, and Frank said, "I have no idea."

Investigation of the Scene
A lamp was tipped over on a table behind the couch, a couch cushion was out of place, a picture on the wall above an easy chair was tilted at a 45 degree angle, and there were newspaper pages and personal papers on the floor.

Evidence Collected
We took pictures of the bruises on Maryann's right forearm, and of the living room. (This is not shown in video.)

Witness Statements
No witness statements. Neighbor was not home when we arrived.

Children Present
Son Timothy, 9, was located at the next door neighbors'. He was not interviewed.

Medical Treatment
Maryann refused medical treatment.

Dangerous Suspect Assessment
911 lists 3 visits to house for domestic disturbance in last 2 years.

Contact Information
(This would be listed on confidential form at booking.)

Disposition
We arrested Frank for domestic assault.

Write the Domestic Violence Report

Conclusion

You should now have the skills to write outstanding reports. You should also be able to use your reports to improve your own police work. If your cases are not being prosecuted, find out why. Were your reports incomplete? Did you break a link in the legal chain? Did you fail to include pertinent facts, or did you fail to collect them?

Other Tips to Improve Your Writing

Re-read and re-write.
After you have written a report, re-read it. Look at each sentence individually and see how many words you can strike out or rewrite. You'll soon find yourself writing better sentences right from the get-go.

Don't panic when you're caught in the "sentence from the black lagoon."
Every writer gets stuck. Ask yourself, "What the heck am I trying to say?" You'll be surprised how often a simple answer presents itself.

Have someone else read your reports.
Everyone needs an editor. Don't be surprised when something that seems perfectly clear to you elicits a big "Huh?" from someone else. This a normal part of writing.

Analyze your weakness.
Which parts of this training were hardest for you? If you feel your grammar skills are lacking, take a class or get a good grammar book. If your legal knowledge is a bit sketchy, find out from your supervisor where you can get more training in your state's laws.

Read.
Someone in your department writes good reports. The more good examples you can read, the sooner you will recognize good writing and be able to imitate it.

Use a checklist.
On the next page is a checklist which covers the basic concepts of this training. Use it to check your reports.

Taking the Post-Test
Before you take the post-test, take a few minutes to review the course. Are there some areas you don't completely understand? You may revisit any online chapter. This will not cause them to revert to an "un-checked" state. When you feel ready, select the Post-Test option from the home page. (You must have completed all the chapters in order to take the test.)

The test questions come from all the chapters. If you miss a question, you will be required to repeat the chapter it came from and retake the post-test. (The chapter or chapters you missed question in will become unchecked again.)

When you have scored 100% on the post-test, you will be notified. Your training officer will be informed by e-mail, and you will receive a certificate of completion. Ready? Good luck!

7 Writing the Domestic Violence Report

Here's a handy checklist to use when reviewing your reports.

Everyday Words
- ❏ "Official sounding" words have been changed to simple words.
- ❏ Unnecessary words have been deleted.
- ❏ Long sentences have been divided into shorter ones.
- ❏ People are identified by name.
- ❏ Pronoun references are clear.
- ❏ Police jargon and codes have been eliminated.

Writing Tips
- ❏ Used "I" or "me" to refer to yourself (once you have stated your name).
- ❏ No incorrect use of "myself."
- ❏ No bad grammar like "I seen," "I been," "I says" or "I go."
- ❏ No extra "dids."
- ❏ Sentences are in active voice.

Organization
- ❏ Paragraphs have one topic.
- ❏ Paragraph topic is stated in the first sentence.
- ❏ Report is in chronological order.

Facts and Details
- ❏ Vague general terms are changed to specific ones.
- ❏ Testimony is attributed to the person who said it.
- ❏ Opinions have been eliminated.
- ❏ All facts are included.
- ❏ Statements of conclusion eliminated (except when needed).

Legal Requirements
- ❏ The crime is described.
- ❏ The sequence of events leading to arrest, citation etc. was described.
- ❏ Used the legal checklist from page 79.
- ❏ Looked for missing links–included all information necessary to proceed with the case.

Special Report Types
DUI/DWI
- ❏ Consulted suggested headings and key points on pages 96-97.

Domestic Violence Report
- ❏ Consulted suggested headings and key points on pages 114-115.

Answers to Practice Exercises

CHAPTER 1

Chapter 1 Exercises 1 - 3

EXERCISE 1 (page 14)

1. Observed — *saw, watched, heard, smelled, felt*
2. Commenced — *began, started*
3. Documented — *wrote, taped, photographed*
4. Multitude — *many*
5. Related — *told, said*
6. Utilized — *used*
7. Ascertained — *learned, asked, saw, found, found out*
8. In reference to — *about, regarding*

EXERCISE 2 (page 14)

1. smelled
2. about, around
3. got out of, left
4. because, stopped
5. called, told
6. used

EXERCISE 3 (page 16)

1. Officer Chandler and I arrived at 1500 York Avenue at 0644. We knocked on the front door. The door was open. There was crying from the back of the house, so we went in to investigate.

2. The driver attempted to stop her car at the intersection of 33rd and Drew Street. The road surface was icy. She was driving over the speed limit. She nearly hit a pedestrian. She slid through a red light.

3. James Rockhold told me he hit his wife. I saw bruises and scratches on her face. I arrested Mr. Rockhold for assault.

Answers

EXERCISE 4 (page 21)

1. I found a jogging suit, duct tape and a pocketknife inside the trunk of the yellow Ford Mustang. I put the pocket knife in a sealed bag for evidence.

   Or:

   I put the jogging suit in a sealed bag for evidence. Or:
   I put the duct tape in a sealed bag for evidence.

2. I asked the passenger to wait in the car and I talked to Jim Fletch about the passenger's behavior.

   Or:

   I asked the passenger to wait in the car and I talked to Jim Fletch about Fletch's behavior.

3. I saw Amy Johnson in the parking lot holding a knife and Jane Bakke mumbling and shuffling slowly in circles. I tried talking to Johnson and did not get a response.

   Or:

   I tried talking to Bakke and did not get a response.

**Chapter 1
Exercise 4**

CHAPTER 2

EXERCISE 1 (page 27)

All the sentences are correct.

EXERCISE 2 (page 27)

1. I
2. me
3. me
4. I

EXERCISE 3 (page 28)

1. I was out there twice to look for evidence. Or,
   I had been out there twice to look for evidence.
2. She went to that club every weekend for two years. Or,
   She had been going to that club every weekend for two years.
3. He said, "Keep your hands off me!"
4. I saw her crying, but she said, "I'm fine, thank you."
5. I said to her, "Ma'am, I need to see your driver's license."

EXERCISE 4 (page 30)

1. confessed
2. said
3. took, broke
4. called

EXERCISE 5 (page 31)

1. turned
2. called
3. said

Answers

EXERCISE 6 (page 32)

On 3/23/2017 at 1950 hours I responded to a domestic at 3397 Irving Avenue North. I arrived at 2002 hours. Officer Farr also arrived at that time. We met the complainant and victim, Alisa Mathews (D.O.B. 12-01-88). She said she and her husband got into an argument, but that everything is OK. She said that he did not hit her. She said he did not even yell at her. She tried to get us to leave the house. Officer Farr and I talked with James Mathews, Alisa's husband. He told us she gets hysterical if she doesn't get her way. He said she threatened to call the cops if he didn't let her keep some clothing she bought. He said he grabbed her by the upper arms and held her back from attacking him. Alisa did not have any injuries or marks on her arms.

EXERCISE 7 (page 34)

1. P
2. P
3. A
4. A
5. P
6. P
7. A
8. P

EXERCISE 8 (page 34)

1. Officer Mader asked the driver for his identification.
2. I patted Johnson down for weapons.
3. I asked Peterson to recite the alphabet.

Chapter 2 Exercises 6-8

CHAPTER 3

EXERCISE 1 (page 40)

1. b
2. d

EXERCISE 2 (page 44)

I was dispatched to 1234 Mulberry Street at 1500 hours on April 10, 2016, regarding a house burglary.

When I got to the house, I met the owner, Patricia Olson. She was standing by the front door. The door was hanging by one hinge and the door frame was splintered. The deadbolt was still in the locked position.

Olson said that she came home after work at about 1430 hours. She did not go into the house when she saw the front door was broken in. She said she went to a neighbor's house to call 911. Olson said her son and husband are out of town on a fishing trip.

I went into the house with my pistol drawn and made a sweep to determine if the person was still inside. I saw two wet, muddy shoe prints on the floor just inside the front door. I saw the back door was open.

In the study, I found the top desk drawer open and several pieces of paper lying on the floor. I called for the evidence technician, John Mikkal, and secured the scene until he arrived.

Olson looked through her things and found that an envelope with about $1600 in cash was missing from the desk. I asked her if she knew who might have taken the cash. She said she had no idea.

Jane Jenson, 1238 Mulberry Street, telephone (555) 234-2349, came up to me at the scene and said she had been home all day. At about 1330 hours she saw a male run from the direction of the Olson house toward the east. She recognized him as Peter Cromley, a friend of the Olson's sixteen-year-old son. Jenson said Cromley lives at 345 2nd Avenue.

Officer Mikkal, the evidence technician, dusted for prints on both the front and back doors and the desk area. No fingerprints were found. He photographed the front door and the shoe prints inside the front door.
I provided Olson with a case number and a Victim's Rights card. I drove to the Cromley house at 345 2nd Avenue to talk to the suspect. I knocked on the door but no one answered.

Answers

CHAPTER 4

EXERCISE 1 (page 51)
1. G
2. S
3. S
4. G
5. S
6. G
7. S
8. S
9. S
10. G
11. S
12. G

**Chapter 4
Exercise 1**

EXERCISE 2 (page 52)

Chapter 4 Exercise 2

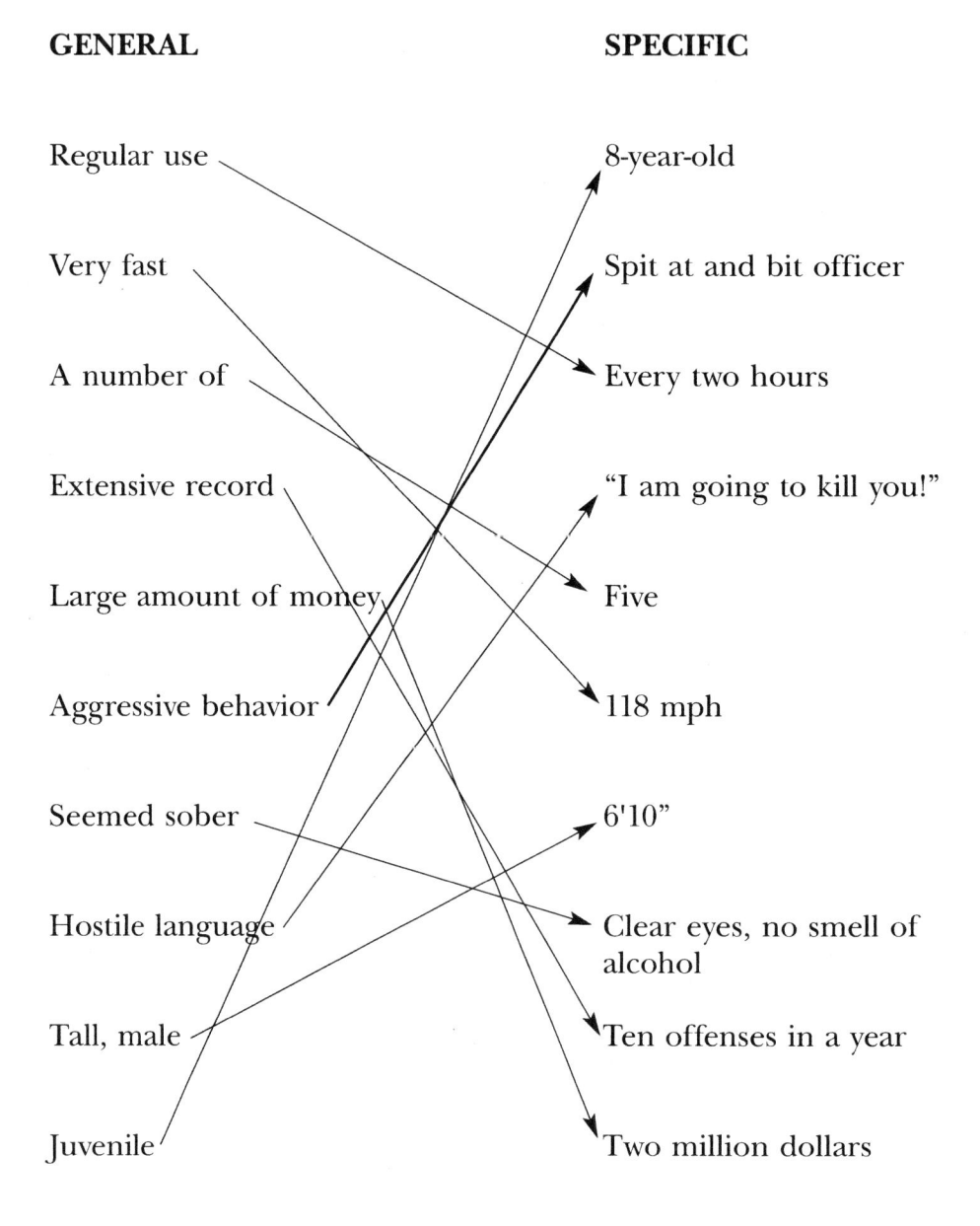

GENERAL	SPECIFIC
Regular use	8-year-old
Very fast	Spit at and bit officer
A number of	Every two hours
Extensive record	"I am going to kill you!"
Large amount of money	Five
Aggressive behavior	118 mph
Seemed sober	6'10"
Hostile language	Clear eyes, no smell of alcohol
Tall, male	Ten offenses in a year
Juvenile	Two million dollars

- Regular use → Every two hours
- Very fast → 118 mph
- A number of → Five
- Extensive record → Ten offenses in a year
- Large amount of money → Two million dollars
- Aggressive behavior → Spit at and bit officer
- Seemed sober → Clear eyes, no smell of alcohol
- Hostile language → "I am going to kill you!"
- Tall, male → 6'10"
- Juvenile → 8-year-old

Answers

EXERCISE 3 (page 55)

(Your answers may vary.)

1. The cash register was open and there was no money in the drawers.

2. Glass was scattered on the floor of the kitchen. A piece of cloth was hanging on the window sill. A footprint was also on the sill.

3. Hardy kicked me and tried to hit me. She swore at me, calling me a "no-good rat-bastard cop." She spit at me.

EXERCISE 4 (page 62)

Directions: Look at the following list. Which items would most likely be inconsequential to a domestic violence report, and thus left out?

___ A lamp was broken and on the floor.

X Dirty dishes were in the sink.

___ The man had scratches on his face.

X It was raining hard.

X The woman was wearing a T-shirt which read "Life's a Bitch and Then You Are One."

X The woman called you a pig while you were interviewing her.

X It was dark outside.

___ The woman was crying.

EXERCISE 5 (page 65)
1. F
2. C
3. C
4. F
5. C
6. C
7. C
8. F
9. C

CHAPTER 5 (page 73)

EXERCISE 1

Your answers may vary.

Chapter 4
Exercises
3-5

Chapter 5
Exercise
1

Simple Word Guide

SIMPLIFY! CLARIFY!

Above-named person(s) . . . . *give the names*

Advised . . . . .said, told

Approximately . . . . .about

Ascertained . . . . .learned

At this point, at that point . . . . .then

At which time... . . . . .then

Commenced . . . . .began, started

Complainant . . . .*consider using name*

Did not pay any attention to . . . . .ignored

Due to the fact that... . . . . .because

Endeavor to ascertain . . . . .try to find out

For the purpose of... . . . . .for

I was unaware of the fact that... . . . . .I did not know...

In addition to... . . . . .besides

In light of the fact that... . . . . .because

In order to... . . . . .to

In the amount of... . . . . .for

In the event that... . . . . .if

In reference to . . . . .about, regarding

In regards to... . . . . .about, regarding, concerning

LERC Report Writing

Extras

Simple Word Guide

In spite of the fact that... ....album, though

In view of... ....since, because

Inasmuch as... ....as, since, because

Made note of... ....noted

Observed ....saw, watched

Prior to... ....before

Put an end to... ....ended

Reached the conclusion... ....concluded

Reporting officer ...."I" *or your name*

Subsequent to... ....after

That ...."that" can usually be deleted

This is the suspect that... ....this suspect... *or give name*

Whereupon ....then

With regard to ....on, about, concerning

131

Sample Report

Sample Report: Robbery

On 6-13-xx at 1745 hours, I was dispatched to 2632 Cleveland Ave. So., and met with the victim, Susan Tastad, regarding a robbery. I also spoke to Joe Mueller, 2638 Cleveland Ave. So., who witnessed part of the robbery.

Tastad said she was putting her bicycle away in the garage behind her house when an unknown man approached her. He pushed her to the garage floor, grabbed her bicycle, and rode off south down the alley behind Cleveland Avenue. Tastad said her elbow was sore from the fall. She also had a 1" scrape on her knee which was pink but not bleeding. She said she did not require medical treatment.

She described the suspect as a white male, around 20 years old, about 6 feet 2 inches, 185 lbs., with shoulder length dark brown hair and a moustache. He was wearing a beige T-shirt, blue jeans, black baseball cap and black boots. Tastad said she would recognize him if she saw him again.

The bicycle is a 2015 white Diamondback Axis mountain bike with front suspension shock absorbers. The bicycle is unlicensed, but has serial #1073456797 on its frame. It has a red nylon rectangular pack about 12" x 5" x 4" on the back rack which contained Tastad's checkbook and wallet. The wallet held Tastad's driver's license, credit cards, and personal items.

Witness Joe Mueller was in his yard in the house north of Tastad's. He heard her scream, ran into the alley, and saw a white male riding south on a bicycle with a red pack on the back. He described the man as about 150 lbs, shoulder length brown hair, with a light-colored T-shirt and blue jeans. He ran to Tastad, who said she had just been robbed. He retrieved her house keys from the garage door, went with her into her house, and called 911.

Tastad was calm during the interview, but kept rubbing her elbow. She again refused medical treatment, but said she would see her doctor if the pain continued. She said her knee felt fine.

I inspected the garage and walked 1 block to the south end of the alley, but found no evidence.

Tastad and Mueller gave me sworn statements. I radioed dispatch the description of the suspect and they transmitted the information to all other units. I gave Tastad a Victim Rights card, and gave my contact card to Mueller. I then drove down the alley and the streets south of 26th Street, but did not see the suspect, the bicycle, or the red pack.

Sample Report: Domestic Violence Short Form
(sometimes called "Matter of Record")

Note: If the officer did not establish probable cause that abuse occurred but an abuse complaint was made, the officer will add a short narrative to the report, explaining the investigation of the claim.

```
Dispatched to a domestic at 123 Main Street on 05/05/xx 22:40 hours. A
caller said she heard screaming and shouting from the apartment below.

Upon arrival, deputies heard yelling coming from the rear of the house
but heard no indications of a physical altercation.

On entry we separated the parties. Sandra Epson (DOB 4-15-59) said
that she and her husband had been arguing over him being fired at work
for excessive absences. Sandra said neither party had threatened or
assaulted the other. She was agitated but did not appear to be injured
or afraid of Kurt Epson (DOB 5-18-60).

Kurt's statement to Deputy Perro was consistent. Both parties were
asked the three risk questions and both said there had been no
previous acts of violence or domestic abuse.

Both parties were warned to keep the noise level down and encouraged
to call the police if either party needed assistance. There was no one
else present in the home.

I checked with 911 who said the caller was asked and did not see or
hear an actual assault. Through the investigation, we determined that
the call was not a domestic abuse situation.
```

LERC *Report Writing*

Example of Police Report Narrative

Example of a Police Report Narrative Worksheet
(provided by St. Tamany Parish, LA Sheriff's Department)

1. **Information provided by 911/dispatch center about this incident:**

2. **Victim Information:**
The victim provided the following account of events:
In response to follow-up questions, the victim further stated that:
Emotional state/demeanor/sobriety:
Injuries:
Other observations related to account of events:

3. **Suspect Information:**
The suspect provided the following account of events:
In response to follow-up questions, the suspect further stated that:
Emotional state/demeanor/sobriety:
Injuries:
Other observations related to account of events:

4. **Witness Information**
Witness(es) _____ provided the following account of events:
Phone Number and Address:
Deputy observations related to witness account of events:

5. **Other Information**
Presence, involvement, and well-being of children:
Presence and involvement of weapon:
Risk Questions:
Suspect's past criminal/protection order history:

6. **Outcomes**
The following actions were taken:
Medical attention:
Additional Notes:
Victim Help Card given to:
Two emergency contacts for victim:

7. **Evidence Collected/Follow-Up Information**
The following photos and/or physical evidence were collected:
Written statements taken from:

SAMPLE

Police Report Narrative

Example of Police Report Narrative

1. Information provided by 911/dispatch center about this incident:

Officer McGarrett and I were dispatched at 16:30 hrs. to 613 Reed Street on a complaint by a child that his father was hitting his mother with a cord. We arrived at 16:37.

2. Victim Information:

I interviewed Sandra Delaney (DOB 5-2-73)

a. Sandra Delaney provided the following account: She came home from work at approximately 5:30 (works at Cub Foods, 800 River Road). Her husband, Jack Delaney, was upset she was late. He began yelling and swearing and accusing her of having an affair. She said she left the living room, went to her bedroom, and Mr. Delaney followed her and again began yelling. She said he began pulling clothes out of the closet and told her to move if she was so unhappy with her family. She tried to leave but he grabbed her. She tried to get out of the room, but Delaney continued to hold her and began hitting her with the extension cord he was holding. She said she yelled at her daughter Jessica (7 yrs.) to go get her brother from the garage. Her son Bryan (16 yrs.) came into the house and started yelling at Delaney to let go of his mother. Delaney let go and said, "Your mother's a tramp, you go ahead and defend her." The daughter called 911.

When I asked Mrs. Delaney about the scratch marks on Jack Delaney, she said she thinks she scratched him when he was holding her in the bedroom. She said this happened about fifteen minutes ago.

b. Emotional state/demeanor/sobriety: Mrs. Delaney was very upset. She appeared to have been crying.

c. Injuries: She had four red lines slightly swelling on the back of her right leg where she says Delaney hit her with the cord. She also had red marks on her right arm and shoulder.

d. Other observations related to account of events: There were a number of shirts and jackets still on their hangers lying on the bedroom floor. Mrs. Delaney said she was also hit on her back but did not want to show it to me. I asked her where the electric cord was and she said he threw it at her in the bedroom. After checking the bedroom, I found a six-foot brown electric cord and collected it as evidence.

3. Suspect Information:

I interviewed Jack Delaney (DOB 12-04-69)

a. Jack Delaney provided the following account of events: He said Mrs. Delaney came home over an hour late from work and refused to talk to him when he asked her where she had been. He asked her several times to talk to him but she refused. He said he followed her into the bedroom and when he raised his voice, she slapped him. He said he then restrained her. He said he did not hit her with the cord. He showed me a scratch mark on his left hand where he said she "clawed me for no reason at all."

b. Emotional state/demeanor/sobriety: Mr. Delaney appeared agitated. He said he had consumed 2 beers that evening. He had a slight odor of alcohol about him. Delaney was continually trying to move within ear shot of his wife.

c. Injuries: I saw a scratch on the back of Mr. Delaney's hand with a small amount of blood.

Sample Report

   d. Other observations related to account of events: He made several attempts to get eye contact with his son Bryan and at one point yelled out to him, "Don't start telling lies for your mother." It appeared to be an attempt to intimidate the boy.

4. **Witness Information**

   a. Witness(es) Jessica and Bryan (ages 7 and 16) provided the following account of events: Jessica, the 7-year-old, said she heard her mother yelling at her father to let go of her and ran out to get her brother. Bryan did not want to talk to me, but said he came into the house to keep things from getting out of control. He would not be specific about what that meant.

   b. Phone Number and Address: Same as victim/suspect. See face sheet.

   c. Deputy observations related to witness account of events: Jessica appeared afraid and shaken-up. She seemed afraid of me and was clinging onto her mother. I decided not to interview either child.

5. **Other Information**

   a. Presence, involvement, and well being of children: It appears that neither child was physically involved in the altercation but could be interviewed at a later date for more details.

   b. Presence and involvement of weapon: No weapons involved in incident. Hunting weapons locked up in back closet.

   c. Risk Questions: I asked Mrs. Delaney about past abuse and she said her husband has been violent in the past. Three years ago he broke her collarbone by hitting her with a broom. That was the worst incident of violence but she said things have been getting worse lately and that Delaney had been drinking heavily since his mother died in the spring. She thought he could "accidentally go too far" because of the drinking. She said Delaney has either hit her, or threatened to, almost weekly over the past six months. She said he doesn't hit the children but he intimidates them and has started getting into grabbing their son when they argue.

   d. Suspect's past criminal/protection order history: Mrs. Delaney said she got a protection order against Mr. Delaney after he broke her collarbone three years ago, but it has since expired. Records check showed no priors but 911 records show three calls to the address in the past 12 months.

6. **Outcomes**

   a. Based on a consideration of the circumstances described in this report, the following actions were taken: I arrested Mr. Delaney for 5th degree assault. I Mirandized him, handcuffed him, and placed him in the squad car.

   b. Medical attention: Refused by both parties.

   c. Additional Notes: On the way to the jail, Delaney made a threat toward Mrs. Delaney, saying, "Someday I'll give that bitch something to call the cops about."

   e. Victim Help Card given to Mrs. Delaney. I also explained to her how to apply for an order for protection, but she said she did not want to separate from her husband.

   f. Two emergency contacts for victim were noted on Request for Commitment form.

7. **Evidence Collected/Follow-Up Information**

   a. The following photos and/or physical evidence were collected: I took photographs of the clothes on the bedroom floor and Mrs. Delaney's leg and arm injuries. I placed the electric cord into evidence.

   b. Written statements taken from: Mrs. Delaney provided me with a written statement; Mr. Delaney refused.

Extras

We hope we have taken some of the pain out of report writing. If you have any suggestions or comments on this workbook or any aspect of the online training, please e-mail us at reportwriting@lerc.com.